A JOHN CATT PUBLICATION

Amarbeer Singh Gill

DUNLOSKY'S
STRENGTHENING THE STUDENT TOOLBOX
IN ACTION

T0198428

IN ACTION SERIES
EDITOR **TOM SHERRINGTON**

WITH ILLUSTRATIONS BY **OLIVER CAVIGLIOLI**

A **WALKTHRUs** PRODUCTION

First published 2022

by John Catt Educational Ltd,
15 Riduna Park, Station Road,
Melton, Woodbridge IP12 1QT

Tel: +44 (0) 1394 389850
Email: enquiries@johncatt.com
Website: www.johncatt.com

© 2022 Amarbeer Singh Gill
Illustrations by Oliver Caviglioli

ISBN: 978 1 915261 26 7

Set and designed by John Catt Educational Limited

TOM SHERRINGTON

The idea for the *In Action* series was developed by John Catt's *Teaching WalkThrus* team after we saw how popular our *Rosenshine's Principles in Action* booklets proved to be. We realised that the same approach might support teachers to access the ideas of a range of researchers, cognitive scientists and educators. A constant challenge that we wrestle with in the world of teaching and education research is the significant distance between the formulation of a set of concepts and conclusions that might be useful to teachers and the moment when a teacher uses those ideas to teach their students in a more effective manner, thereby succeeding in securing deeper or richer learning. Sometimes so much meaning is lost along that journey, through all the communication barriers that line the road, that the implementation of the idea bears no relation to the concept its originator had in mind. Sometimes it's more powerful to hear from a teacher about how they implemented an idea than it is to read about the idea from a researcher or cognitive scientist directly – because they reduce that distance; they push some of those barriers aside.

In our *In Action* series, the authors and their collaborative partners are all teachers or school leaders close to the action in classrooms in real schools. Their strategies for translating their subjects' work into practice bring fresh energy to a powerful set of original ideas in a way that we're confident will support teachers with their professional learning and, ultimately, their classroom practice. In doing so, they are also paying their respects to the original researchers and their work. In education, as in so many walks of life, we are standing on the shoulders of giants. We believe that our selection of featured researchers and papers represents some of the most important work done in the field of education in recent times.

In this book we have a classic *In Action* pairing: the research presented by John Dunlosky in his popular paper "Strengthening the student toolbox" and the practice and classroom experience of maths teacher Amarbeer Singh Gill. I had not met Amarbeer until he approached me with the idea of adding this book to the series, but after our initial discussion it was an easy decision – his enthusiasm for Dunlosky's ideas was evident from the start and it's been a real joy to play a small part in bringing the book to life. Dunlosky's short "toolbox" paper explores a range of research in a wonderfully evaluative manner, explicitly interrogating the extent to which a set of contender ideas translate into improved learning. Not all the contenders are as successful as people might think or hope; this kind of reality check helps us to develop our capacity for intelligent research engagement. In this book, Amarbeer guides us skilfully through each of the strategies, exploring why they work in terms of cognitive science and then how to apply them in practice. As Dunlosky highlights in his foreword, Amarbeer has done a superb job of placing the research into real classroom contexts that bring all the ideas to life.

Finally, in producing this series, we would like to acknowledge the significant influence of the researchED movement run by Tom Bennett that started in 2013. I was present at the first conference and, having seen the movement grow over the intervening years, I feel that many of us, including several *In Action* authors, owe a significant debt of gratitude to researchED for providing the forum where teachers' and researchers' ideas and perspectives can be shared. We are delighted, therefore, to be contributing a share of the royalties to researchED to support them in their ongoing non-profit work.

FOREWORD

JOHN DUNLOSKY

Imagine embracing carpentry as a new hobby because you are excited to build furniture. You begin by purchasing a hammer and a screwdriver. And, of course, you'll need a saw and many other tools as you proceed, such as a lathe to make round legs, sandpaper of all grain sizes to make everything smooth, and all sorts of glue and paint to finish your projects. Each of these tools will be useful, but some are more general and can be used to solve many problems (such as your hammer), whereas others are speciality tools made to help you solve very specific problems. To be a great carpenter, you not only need to know when to use each tool, but also how to use each one to make the finest furniture.

The same is true of the strategies that instructors and students use when they are trying to meet various learning objectives – strategies like completing practice exam questions, reading (and rereading) assigned chapters, developing mental images or even highlighting passages in a textbook. Just like a carpenter's toolbox, the majority of the strategies that are commonly in a student's strategy toolbox can help them to meet their objectives. Nevertheless, all strategies are not made equal: some can lead to effective learning in many contexts, whereas others are specialised and meant for specific contexts. For instance, retrieval practice can be harnessed to boost students' memory, comprehension and retention of many different kinds of materials, whereas mental imagery is most useful for a small subset of materials (that can be imagined) and, even then, only for students who can generate mental images. Any given strategy can be useful to most students, but only when it is used appropriately and at the right time.

In this volume, Amarbeer Singh Gill provides a super tutorial on various strategies that all have their place in a student's toolbox. Even better, the strategies are inexpensive if not cost-free, so any instructor or student can take advantage of their power. Nevertheless, for the strategies to be used effectively, instructors and students need to know when and how to use them, and Amarbeer provides insights into why the various strategies work and when and how to use them. What I found particularly enlightening were all the creative recommendations on using these strategies and the emphasis that a strategy in and of itself is rarely "good" or "bad", but it is how that strategy is used that makes the difference. For this reason alone, I can highly recommend this volume – it provides tangible guidance on how students can use the strategies while studying on their own and how they can be adapted for use in your classroom.

Strengthening the Student Toolbox In Action will give you concrete ideas on how to harness the power of effective strategies for your students, and it is a superbly written volume that is accessible and fun to read. I know you will come away with great ideas to put into practice immediately, so grab your favourite highlighter and get ready to build your strategy toolbox!

John Dunlosky is a professor of psychological sciences and the director of the Science of Learning and Education (SOLE) Center at Kent State University, Ohio

ACKNOWLEDGEMENTS

Pedd mundha-hoo cut-ee-ah tis dal suk-un-deh
When the tree is cut off at its roots, the branches wither and die[1]

No achievement is ever made in isolation. We can enjoy the fruits of trees now only because they were planted before our time. In appreciating the fruits, it behoves us to remember those who laid the seeds, nurtured the plant, and had the foresight and selflessness to build something even though they may not ultimately have had the chance to enjoy the results. And so, reflecting on this process, I find myself reflecting on my own roots. This book is not just the culmination of my own writing and research; it's the culmination of the bravery and humility of those who came before me and continue to support me today. In particular, my grandparents and parents, who built and continue to build the life I enjoy today; my brother, who always looks out for me and provides me with just the right amount of distraction when I need it; my Bhooa Ji, who has always celebrated my achievements as if they were her own; and my wife, whose support and encouragement have been invaluable. Thank you to them also for their time and words of wisdom during the creation of this book. There are many other family members, friends and colleagues whom I've had the privilege of knowing and haven't mentioned here; know that I am the sum of our interactions and your encouragement, advice and support were and always will be greatly appreciated.

We stand on the shoulders of others and so thanks must be given to all the teachers, educators and researchers whose work has helped this book come to fruition. Thank you to Alex Sharratt and Tom Sherrington for taking a shot on a maths teacher from Gravesend and giving this project the green light. Special thanks to Tom for doing such a great job of treading the line between guidance and autonomy, and allowing me to take ownership of the writing. Thank you to Oliver Caviglioli for his illustrations, and to Jonathan Barnes and Isla McMillan for their help with the editing process. Thank you to Peps Mccrea, Emma Lark, Nick Rose, Kyle Bailey, Jon Hutchinson and Steve Farndon, who set me on the path of evidence-informed practice, and to Peps and Nick for their feedback on this book. Thank you to Kirstie Dixon for her fantastic case study contribution, and to Jessica Appleton for sharing her invaluable time, expertise and case study from a primary classroom. Lastly, thank you of course to John Dunlosky for his very generous foreword, his support for this project, and for putting the fantastic "toolbox" paper together and allowing it to be shared with educators across the world. I hope it continues to improve the knowledge and practice of teachers everywhere, and that this book acts as a helpful companion to the original work.

TABLE OF CONTENTS

INTRODUCTION

'It's the night before her biology exam, and the high school
student has just begun to study'[2]

This quote is the opening line of Dunlosky's paper. You may be able to relate to this line yourself, and if you're a teacher I'm quite certain many of your students will relate to it as well. I think this line gets to the core of Dunlosky's paper: learning is a process we all have to go through, but are we doing it effectively? The next lines in the paper describe the student highlighting and rereading passages in her textbook – again, something we teachers and our students have done on many occasions. You may even have a highlighter with you right now! It's this common experience that makes Dunlosky's paper so powerful. Before you move on to the next chapters in this book, I recommend that you read through the original paper – another of its selling points is that it's a very easy read. The QR code and URL at the end of this introduction will take you straight there.

The purpose of this book is to consider the paper's findings, the underlying mechanisms to help us understand these findings, and examples of how the findings can be put to effective use in the classroom. Although the intention of Dunlosky's paper is to impart successful learning strategies to students, we're going to explore how we can use the "toolbox" from a teacher's perspective. The book is split into three chapters: the first considers key aspects of the paper, explores the classification system used by Dunlosky, and provides a (brief!) introduction to the science of learning that puts his work into context; the second looks directly at Dunlosky's strategy recommendations and considers classroom examples, theory and the potential limitations of those strategies; the final chapter presents some key ideas to bear in mind when implementing changes to teaching practice. I hope this book does justice to Dunlosky's original work and, most importantly, I hope it helps to translate his work into classrooms, so we can help our students to achieve the best outcomes.

To close this introduction, let's think about how we can forge a fruitful link between research and practice. A colleague of mine once said, "The only thing worse than a bad idea is a good idea badly implemented." Teachers operate in a high-stakes environment where a huge number of variables are outside our control, but one thing we *can* control is what we do in our classrooms. In seeking to improve our practice, we must acknowledge the impact we can have on the life outcomes of our students. Because of this, patience and caution must be our watchwords: we must first understand why solutions might be fit for purpose, by exploring research and looking at the basis and limitations of the ideas we're trying to implement. Adopting this approach will make it more likely that we – and, more importantly, our students – can enjoy the fruits of our labour.

bit.ly/JDunlosky

CHAPTER 1

UNDERSTANDING DUNLOSKY

'If simple techniques were available that teachers and students could use to improve student learning and achievement, would you be surprised if teachers were not being told about these techniques and if many students were not using them?'[3]

To have our students leave school with more knowledge than when they started is the key goal of education. The question, however, is: are we doing this effectively? Given that schools and teachers are time-poor, are we helping teachers to use that time in the most efficient way?

These are the questions that Dunlosky and a group of colleagues set out to answer. How can we work around the existing demands of teaching and achieve the best learning for our students? A key goal for the researchers was that actual teachers should be able to implement their recommendations in actual classrooms. Although the "toolbox" paper was authored by Dunlosky, it's a summary of a project that also involved several of his colleagues. The quote that opens this chapter is taken from that project, which considers each of the strategies in greater detail.

In the first part of this chapter, we'll look at the unique features of Dunlosky's paper and that wider project that make them such valuable resources for teachers and students in answering the questions at the start of this chapter. We'll consider what makes Dunlosky's paper special, the different aspects of the recommendations and the classification process used. We'll conclude this chapter by exploring a few ideas about learning that can help us to understand each strategy in context.

Part 1: The research

Preferences

'We chose to review some strategies ... because students reported using them often yet we wondered about their effectiveness'[4]

I often find that students might not have a ruler, protractor or even a spare pen in their pencil case, but they almost always have a highlighter. And when exam season arrives, they make sure they get their money's worth: in the words of one former colleague, "They might as well have used a paintbrush."

Dunlosky and his colleagues made a point of reviewing strategies that are regularly used by students and teachers alike. They looked at what students frequently do when studying and asked: is this the best way? The findings make for very interesting reading, revealing a gap between the strategies that are used most frequently and those that are most effective.

As teachers, we know this is hugely significant. With the help of Dunlosky's paper, we're able to guide students not only towards more effective strategies but also away from less effective ones.

Usage

'Our intent was to survey strategies that teachers could coach students to use without sacrificing too much class time and that any student could use'[5]

The researchers' key criteria for choosing the strategies was that students and teachers should be able to use them with no additional materials apart from some basic stationery. Given the hectic nature of schooling for both students and teachers, this is crucial. As teachers, we face a huge number of demands on our time and it's rare that we're in a position where we can prioritise *how* to learn over *what* to learn. Left to their own devices, students will likely choose strategies like highlighting, rereading and summarising because they *feel* easier. They make us feel like we're learning: we read a bit of text and are able to immediately recall all of it. But, as we'll see, this knowledge is short-lived and lulls us into a false sense of security. Conversely, strategies like testing are hard: we must put in more effort and we do get things wrong, so it can feel like we're not learning as effectively as if we had just read the information.

Steering students away from poor study strategies and towards better ones is no small task. Some schools have made a concerted effort by providing students with study skills sessions. However, changing habits is incredibly difficult (as those who have attempted to keep a new year's resolution can confirm) and so it's unlikely that these sessions will have the intended impact without being an embedded part of the everyday teaching that students receive. Three factors that can aid habit formation are repetition, stable conditions and rewards.[6] As teachers, we can use these factors alongside the strategies from Dunlosky's paper to aid student learning in three ways:

1. By regularly coaching students in the proper use of the strategies.

2. By setting tasks and tailoring our curriculum to be compatible with the strategies.

3. By regularly incorporating them into our own teaching.

The second suggestion will require some hard thinking: we may have to sacrifice some parts of the curriculum to ensure others are properly embedded. As Dylan Wiliam writes, "if our curriculum is to be broad and balanced, we have to leave out important elements of the curriculum, in order to create more time for the even more important elements".[7] Achieving any one of the points above will help our students; achieving all of them will set students up for success not only while they are in our classrooms, but throughout a lifetime of learning.

Classification

'An aim of this monograph is to encourage students to use the appropriate learning technique (or techniques) to accomplish a given instructional objective'[8]

It's often the case in education (and in life) that we want to place things into simple dichotomies: good and bad, easy and hard, slow and fast, etc. Dunlosky makes a concerted effort in his paper to avoid these polarising categorisations and instead rates the strategies on a spectrum of effectiveness. In my opinion, Dunlosky's paper does a great job of taking expert research and making it accessible to teachers by expressing it in everyday language and relating it directly to classroom practice. As one blog post about the paper puts it, "experts can also bring common sense to suggestions about implementation".[9] Dunlosky and his colleagues sought to identify which strategies could be implemented in classrooms to best serve a particular purpose, at a particular time, in a particular context. In order to get the most out of the strategies, we must take the time to be aware of the purposes, times and contexts to ensure we select the most appropriate one.

Dunlosky classifies the strategies as:

- Most effective learning strategies.
- Strategies with much promise.
- Less useful strategies (that students use a lot).

These classifications reflect the robustness of the available evidence in support of each strategy and how generalisable each strategy is across four categories: the types of materials used for study (e.g. diagrams, vocabulary, etc.); the learning conditions (reading vs listening, group vs individual learning, etc.); the characteristics of the students (age, prior knowledge, ability, etc.); and the tasks used to measure outcomes (free recall, problem-solving, essay-writing, etc.). The two strategies rated as most effective are supported by highly robust evidence and are highly generalisable. Other strategies have been placed in the remaining two categories for a range of reasons, such as: their use is limited to a small number of materials; they are only shown to work with specific student characteristics; or insufficient evidence was available at the time to give them a higher rating.

Exemplifying the 'spectrum of effectiveness'

Let's look at two strategies at opposite ends of the effectiveness spectrum to try to illustrate the classification process: practice testing (most effective) and highlighting (less useful).

Practice testing

Testing is a word that is rarely met with cheers, and it's something most school-age students do not welcome. However, *practice* testing is rated by Dunlosky and his colleagues as one of the two most effective study strategies (I emphasise the "practice" aspect here and will unpack this in chapter 2). Practice testing has been shown to have positive learning effects for:

- A range of formats including free recall (e.g. blank-sheet retrieval), cued recall (e.g. responses to a question), fill-in-the-blank and multiple-choice-style questions.
- Comprehension (on top of recall) as well as some procedural tasks (e.g. resuscitation procedures[10]) and tasks that involve predicting future

outcomes (e.g. an input-output function[11]). Furthermore, there is evidence of benefits to learning even when the format of the practice testing doesn't match the end test[12] (e.g. the practice uses free recall and the final test uses multiple-choice or a short paragraph).

- A wide variety of ages, from nursery/kindergarten students all the way up to university students and even beyond with middle-aged and older adults.[13]

- Individuals with varying levels of prior knowledge and with varying levels of ability (one study showed an impact for people with Alzheimer's disease and other memory impairments).[14]

- A range of subjects and topics including languages, general knowledge, scientific and historical facts, arithmetic, spellings and definitions. Alongside these verbal materials, benefits have also been shown for visual or spatial information such as: features of maps, animals and plants; locations of objects; and symbols.[15]

- A range of retention intervals, ranging from a few minutes to weeks, months and, in some cases, years.[16]

- Real-life educational contexts and materials (i.e. in actual classrooms with curriculum materials rather than in lab conditions with constructed materials).[17]

Dunlosky and his colleagues tested this strategy's applicability across a vast array of measures, finding multiple sources of evidence demonstrating impact and more than 100 years of significant evidence to back up their categorisation of practice testing as an effective strategy.[18]

Highlighting and underlining

On the opposite end of the spectrum are highlighting and underlining. Some readers may be keenly highlighting or underlining this very book, so I'll begin this section with some reassurance: Dunlosky definitely doesn't urge us to throw our highlighters away and stop underlining. This is why it's helpful to think of these strategies on a spectrum of effectiveness, rather than simply as "good" or "bad". If our purpose is to pick out key information from a text and make it easy to locate later then highlighting is a perfectly good strategy to use. However, if our goal is to retain information for later recall then we'll likely be better served by a different strategy.

Dunlosky and his colleagues not only found little evidence demonstrating the benefits of highlighting or underlining on learning, but also a number of studies that demonstrated "no benefit of highlighting (as it is typically used) over and above the benefit of simply reading".[19] The researchers determined that this strategy wasn't widely applicable across their criteria and in some cases was detrimental to making inferences within a chapter of text.[20] It's also limited to written materials, particularly prose-friendly materials.

It's worth making one point explicit: **practice testing isn't "good", just as highlighting isn't "bad"**. It could even be argued that practice testing done really poorly may be worse than highlighting done really well. The aim of this book is to light a path towards good use of these strategies and offer a starting point for further investigation, before we take the strategies into our classrooms and refine them to achieve the best outcomes for our students.

Takeaways: the strategies

- Knowing which strategies are more/less effective puts us in a better place to support our students.

- We should think hard about what we want to prioritise and what we may need to sacrifice in order to do so.

- The strategies discussed by Dunlosky can be used in a wide variety of subjects and situations.

- Each strategy can be appropriate for a given purpose, in a given context.

- There are very few "bad" strategies, but there are many bad uses for any given strategy.

- Each strategy is classified based on the strength of the evidence around it and the situations it could be used in.

Part 2: An introduction to the science of learning

Dunlosky and his colleagues include a section on the theoretical arguments for why each strategy should work.[21] This helps us to get a better grasp on the key aspects of the strategies and how they can be applied in the classroom. In this part, we'll look at some key concepts and terms to connect the theory of the strategies to how and why they can work in our classrooms.

What is learning?

> 'Learning ... [is] the more or less permanent change in knowledge or understanding'[22]

Our goal as teachers is to ensure our students learn – and retain that learning for as long as possible. But, in order to meet this goal, we need to first define what we mean by "learning". If we teach a student how to solve equations and later in that same lesson they answer an equations question correctly, would we say this technique has been learned? If we teach a student how to use French verbs in the present tense and they do this successfully in a new context outside the classroom, would we call this learning? At what point can we say our goal has been achieved?

Although there are various definitions of learning, in this book we'll use the definition above, from Robert and Elizabeth Bjork, which emphasises the idea of *permanence*. Therefore, we wouldn't describe the student solving equations as having "learned" this technique – not yet! If they were able to demonstrate the technique after a significant delay, or in various contexts, then we could be more confident in saying that the knowledge had been learned. But learning is an invisible process, something we can only infer based on what we see students *do* – their performance.[23] This raises an important question: how is it that students can demonstrate the thing we're teaching them, even though they haven't yet learned it? How is it that they can seemingly "get it" in one lesson, only to "lose it" by the next?

A model that can help when answering questions like these is Daniel Willingham's model of memory,[24] illustrated on the next page by Oliver Caviglioli.

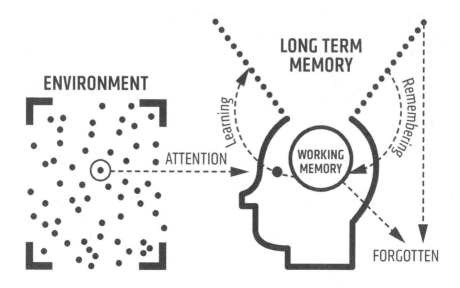

We can only learn what we pay attention to.[25] Once we've directed our attention, information can be processed in our working memory (WM), the part of our mind where conscious thinking takes place.[26] Long-term memory (LTM) is where all our knowledge (of facts like 2 x 6 = 12 and of procedures such as how to ride a bike) is stored, unconsciously, until it's needed and enters our working memory, where we become aware of it.[27] For example, if I ask "What colour stripes do zebras have?" you would fairly easily answer "Black and white". We all possess this information but it lies dormant in our LTM. When your attention is directed, however, you process the question in your WM and bring that particular bit of information from your LTM to your WM, becoming aware of it.

Our WM has a very limited capacity: it can only handle about four "chunks" of information at one time and is easily overloaded.[28] However, our LTM can help with this. It's not a "hard drive" that passively has information saved on to it; rather, it actively supports WM by organising new information into larger and larger chunks.[29] So, although we can still only deal with about four chunks of information at once, the size of those chunks can vary significantly – for example, the word "cat" for most adults is likely to be one chunk, but for people learning to read English for the first time, each individual letter will be one chunk. Well-learned information will be deeply embedded in LTM and can quickly be brought into WM. In addition to this, the more knowledge we have in our LTM, the easier it is to learn new knowledge, because instead of learning

20

new ideas in isolation we're able to integrate them into existing knowledge.[30] Therefore, having deep and well-embedded knowledge in LTM should be a fundamental goal of teaching, as not only are we consolidating what students already know, but we're also making it easier for them to learn even more.

Peps Mccrea offers an analogy to help us make sense of some aspects of WM and LTM: if we consider our LTM to be a map, our WM is the pencil we use to draw in new paths and edit old ones.[31] When we teach students new information, their WM makes faint outlines of new paths; because these initial outlines are faint, if they aren't revisited they become harder to access in future. It's only with *purposeful* practice (we'll unpack this idea in chapter 2) that the initial outlines are etched deeper into our LTM map, making the paths easier to find and navigate the next time we need them. This purposeful practice is what leads to changes in LTM and thus learning.

Crucially, the processes that lead to learning are *effortful*. Thinking hard about the new information in WM, trying to apply it or integrate with prior knowledge, or retrieving something from our LTM are all effortful processes. As we'll see in chapter 2, rereading is not an effective study strategy precisely because it can be done passively, without effort. In order to learn, we must engage in effortful practice. But, as Dunlosky shows, not all practice is equal.

We just went over this yesterday – how have they forgotten it already?

'Forgetting is both endemic and predictable'[32]

The title of this section is a classic teacher thought and a regular conversation between colleagues at break times. To teachers, forgetting can be highly frustrating, even a nemesis at times. But forgetting plays a crucial role in learning and understanding how it works will allow us to maximise its impact.

In the first experiment known to track the rate of forgetting,[33] Hermann Ebbinghaus studied groups of letters and found that his ability to successfully recall them declined rapidly,[34] even within a single hour (see figure 1 on the next page). This finding was hugely significant, demonstrating that **forgetting is inevitable and should be expected.**

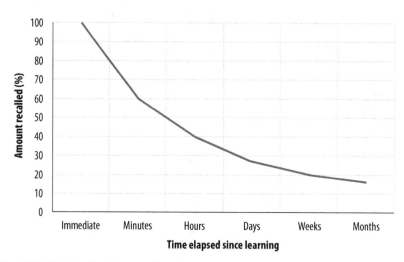

Figure 1. The Ebbinghaus forgetting curve.[35]

Building on this, the Bjorks described any memory as having two properties: a retrieval strength (how easily accessible it is from LTM) and a storage strength (how deeply embedded it is in LTM).[36] Storage strength relates to how "long-lasting" our memories are, how well we can maintain them even if we don't use them for a while, and is presumed to only be accumulative – i.e. it can only get stronger.[37] Retrieval strength, however, can fluctuate – i.e. it can get stronger or weaker. Retrieval strength will be high for new learning but can decline rapidly, and disuse over time is a factor that can lead to reductions.[38] As we know, well-learned information is deeply embedded in LTM and can quickly be brought into WM. We can now build on this knowledge and say that well-learned information is deeply embedded in our LTM as it has *high storage strength*, and can be quickly brought into our WM as it has *high retrieval strength*.

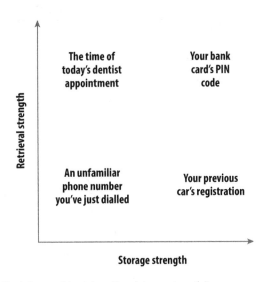

Figure 2. The interaction between retrieval strength and storage strength.[39]

Figure 2 gives some concrete examples of how these two strengths interact. Your PIN is something that's very well learned: you can recall it easily right now and would likely still be able to do so even after a significant gap (high retrieval strength and high storage strength). Conversely, when you've just dialled an unfamiliar phone number you're unlikely to be able to recall it a short while later, even with the help of some cues (low retrieval strength and low storage strength). A few cues will help you to recall the registration number of your previous car because this information is likely pretty well embedded (low retrieval strength and high storage strength), and after your visit to the dentist you don't need to hold on to the time of the appointment, so it will be hard to remember afterwards even if you do have some cues (high retrieval strength and low storage strength).

This is why it can appear as if students have "got it" when they answer questions correctly and demonstrate understanding during new learning; the recency of the learning and the large amount of cues available mean retrieval strength is high. It also explains why students can appear to have "lost it" only a few days later: new learning has low storage strength, forgetting is inevitable and the students haven't had an opportunity to practise, so the retrieval strength has declined rapidly. In other words, the information had not been truly learned – the change in knowledge was temporary, not permanent. All is not lost, however. Surprisingly, lower retrieval strengths can benefit us in the long run – something we'll unpack in chapter 2.

Takeaways: how we learn

- Memory is split into two components:

  - Working memory – the site of "thinking". Has limited capacity.
  - Long-term memory – where knowledge is stored. Supports WM by organising information into "chunks".

- Memories can be thought of as having two strengths: retrieval strength and storage strength.
- Forgetting is inevitable – we should expect it and plan accordingly.
- Learning is an effortful process that takes time and purposeful practice.
- Learning is a permanent change in knowledge or understanding.

Further reading

Bjork, E.L. & Bjork, R.A. (2011) "Making things hard on yourself, but in a good way: creating desirable difficulties to enhance learning", in M.A. Gernsbacher et al. (eds.) *Psychology and the Real World: essays illustrating fundamental contributions to society*, Worth Publishers

Didau, D. & Rose, N. (2016) *What Every Teacher Needs to Know About Psychology*, John Catt Educational

Dunlosky, J. (2013) "Strengthening the student toolbox: study strategies to boost learning", *American Educator*, 37:3, 12-21

Dunlosky, J., Rawson, K., Marsh, E., Nathan, M. & Willingham, D. (2013) "Improving students' learning with effective learning techniques: promising directions from cognitive and educational psychology", *Psychological Science in the Public Interest*, 14:1, 4-58

Kirschner, P., Sweller, J. & Clark, R. (2006) "Why minimal guidance during instruction does not work: an analysis of the failure of constructivist, discovery, problem-based, experiential, and inquiry-based teaching", *Educational Psychologist*, 41:2, 75-86

Mccrea, P. (2017) *Memorable Teaching*

Willingham, D.T. (2009) "Why don't students like school? Because the mind is not designed for thinking", *American Educator*, Spring, 4-13

CHAPTER 2

THE STRATEGIES

In chapter 1, we explored what makes Dunlosky's paper special and how he classified each strategy, as well as framing the paper in the context of the science of learning. In this chapter, we'll use those ideas to unpack the strategies, the theory behind why they work, ideas for classroom usage and potential limitations to bear in mind. Although Dunlosky and his colleagues carried out research on 10 different strategies (see figure 3), in the "toolbox" paper some strategies were grouped together because of the overlap between them. Therefore, this book follows the "toolbox" paper's breakdown of strategies.

Technique	Extent and conditions of effectiveness
Practice testing	Very effective in a wide array of situations.
Distributed practice	Very effective in a wide array of situations.
Interleaved practice	Promising for maths and concept learning, but needs more research.
Elaborative interrogation	Promising, but needs more research.
Self-explanation	Promising, but needs more research.
Rereading	Distributed rereading can be helpful, but time could be better spent using another strategy.
Highlighting and underlining	Not particularly helpful, but can be used as a first step toward further study.
Summarisation	Helpful only with training in how to summarise.
Keyword mnemonic	Somewhat helpful for learning languages, but benefits are short-lived.
Imagery for text	Benefits are limited to imagery-friendly text; needs more research.

Figure 3. All the strategies reviewed by Dunlosky and his colleagues.[40]

Part 1: Most effective learning strategies
Practice testing

'Retrieval practice is possibly the most effective way of retaining knowledge and yet this discovery is often used poorly in schools with testing being used as the final endpoint in a process of learning as opposed to a means of facilitating learning along the journey'[41]

What is practice testing?

In one experiment,[42] students were given a passage of text to read and were told they would later be tested on that text. They would all have four opportunities to study the text and were put into one of three conditions: four reading sessions (SSSS), three reading sessions followed by a practice test (SSST), and one reading session followed by three practice tests (STTT). The test sessions simply involved students being asked to recall as much as they could about the text. This meant that the students who reread the text had multiple opportunities to revisit 100% of the material, whereas the students in the STTT group could only revisit whatever they could recall, likely less than 100%.

All the groups were tested five minutes after their final session or test, and then again one week later. The results are illustrated in figure 4.

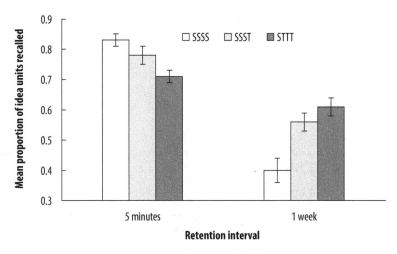

Figure 4. Student performance on immediate and delayed retention tests after learning text passages.[43]

In the test five minutes afterwards, the SSSS group outperformed both other groups. However, after a delay of just one week we can see the significant decline in performance of the SSSS group, versus the relatively smaller decline in the STTT group.

If we don't utilise the benefits of practice testing on learning, we miss out on one of the most robust and widely applicable strategies to enhance learning. The key to this strategy – which goes by many other names, including quizzing and retrieval practice – is any activity that asks students to retrieve target knowledge from their memory. Dunlosky suggests such activities could take the form of:

- Blank-sheet retrieval, e.g. "Write down everything you know about…".
- Cued recall such as fill-in-the-blank exercises or multiple-choice quizzes.
- Completing a short essay where students have to retrieve knowledge from memory.[44]

Dunlosky suggests that the biggest gains come from activities that require more recall rather than recognition, but that any retrieval is better than none. Practice testing can also highlight to students what knowledge needs to be revisited, should they fail to correctly recall the target knowledge.

Dunlosky and his colleagues make a point of emphasising the use of the word "practice" for this strategy,[45] emphasising the need for low stakes or no stakes, without grades or consequences such as results contributing to report cards or summative grades. Without fail, every time I've asked a colleague "What's the first thing a student does when they get a piece of work back with a score/grade on it?" the answer is: "Look at the grade and compare with their friends." This is something we want to try rigorously to avoid.

If we place emphasis on the result, we reinforce the idea of practice testing as an endpoint rather than as a tool for learning. We may also lull students into a false sense of security: they may think that because they have scored highly they have "learned" the material. But, as we discussed in chapter 1, forgetting is inevitable and without practice that information will be forgotten. So, instead, we should ensure students have the opportunity to recall each item correctly at least once, providing feedback where necessary.[46]

Why does practice testing work?

'[Memory is] the residue of thought, meaning that the more you think about something, the more likely it is that you'll remember it later'[47]

Let's go back to the experiment discussed in the previous section: why is it that the students in the SSSS group scored so well immediately after their study, but their performance fell so dramatically after a relatively short delay? And, conversely, why did the performance of the students in the STTT group not suffer to the same extent? One suggestion is that "information retrieved becomes more retrievable in the future".[48] Each search in our LTM for target information will involve recalling related information, and the process of recalling related information will create more ways to access the target information in the future.[49] To return to Peps Mccrea's analogy discussed in chapter 1, when we think about something new, our WM (the pencil) either draws new routes on to or edits old routes in our LTM (the map). Each time we retrieve knowledge from our LTM, it's etched even deeper and stays that way for longer after each test; navigating our map becomes quicker.[50]

This process of searching in LTM is effortful. The students in the STTT group were engaging in effortful practice each time by searching their LTM, so they were reaping the benefits of retrieval. The students in the SSSS group were not engaging in this effortful practice because reading can be done passively, so the students couldn't reap those benefits. We can also think about this experiment in terms of retrieval and storage strength. In the SSSS group there was high retrieval strength immediately after the study sessions, but this had declined rapidly by the time of the delayed test. Among the STTT group, the retrieval strength wasn't as high initially for all the information, but it didn't decline so precipitously because the act of retrieval increases storage strength, while increased storage strength slows the decay in retrieval strength.[51]

How can we use practice testing in the classroom?

Essentially, practice testing can involve any low-stakes or no-stakes activity that requires students to retrieve knowledge from memory (so it must be a closed-book activity that includes no or minimal cues/prompts). Here are some ideas for how you can bring practice testing into your classroom.

- Incorporate a short quiz into each lesson:

  - Quizzes can be short-answer, multiple-choice, true/false or involve demonstrating working (e.g. in maths or science).

  - Students can apply labels to a blanked-out diagram or identify/recognise images.

  - Students can reproduce quotes, definitions or lists of keywords/facts/vocabulary.

- Use flashcards:

  - Put the keyword/idea on one side of the flashcard and the relevant information on the other.

  - Get students to look at the keyword/idea and write down the relevant information.

  - Use the back of the flashcard to check accuracy and correct if necessary.

  - If the answer is incorrect, move the card to the back of the pile so there's another opportunity to practise within the same session.

- Try diminishing-cues retrieval practice[52] (see the languages example on page 31).

- When getting students to take notes in class, encourage them to leave space at the bottom or on the other side of the page. They can cover up their notes (or sections of them) and quiz themselves in the blank space.

- Do a "brain dump" (also called blank-sheet retrieval). Get students to write down everything they can remember about a given topic.

- In **English**, a key part of the literature exam is remembering key quotes from *Macbeth*. Having covered the material, some of the methods above could be used to help students retain those key quotes.

- In **science**, use starter questions such as:

  - What would be the products of a reaction between an acid and a metal carbonate?

- Write down definitions of key terms such as nucleus, monomer, polymer, vacuole, etc.
- What is the symbol equation for aerobic respiration?

▫ Give students diagrams or equations with key information blanked out or only partially given so students have to fill in the rest:

- An image of a plant/animal cell where students are required to label all the features. The image might act as a cue – parts of the image could be gradually removed, with students asked to draw and label a complete diagram as competence develops.
- Add the missing information to complete the equation for photosynthesis: $6CO_2 + \_\_\_\_ \rightarrow C_6H_{12}O_6 + \_\_\_\_$

- In **maths**, students need to know various area equations for their GCSE exams. A blanked-out formulae sheet that students have to fill in can act as a form of practice testing.
- In **PE**, target technical knowledge by using:

▫ Short questions such as "What are the three body types and their features?" or "What is the definition of cardiovascular endurance?"

▫ Blank-sheet retrieval activities with tasks such as "Name as many components of fitness as you can".

▫ Multiple-choice questions such as:

Identify the equation to work out cardiac output.

a. Blood pressure × heart rate.

b. Stroke volume × heart rate.

c. Blood pressure × stroke volume.

d. Tidal volume × stroke volume.

- **Drama**:

▫ Set a quiz with questions that target technical knowledge – for example, "Name at least three physical skills that we can use to convey information about a character" or "What is the difference between a downlight and a backlight?"

▫ You could take this even further as a blank-sheet retrieval activity, asking students to note down as much information as possible about the topic – for example, "Write down as many physical skills as you can think of and a definition or description for each one."

- **Languages**:
  - Start with a study section where students have full vocabulary pairs:
    - Apple = manzana
    - Orange = naranja
    - To eat = comer
    - To drink = beber
  - Then have an initial practice section where one letter is removed:
    - Apple = m_nzana
    - Orange = n_ranja
    - To eat = c_mer
    - To drink = b_ber
  - In further practice sections, remove one letter each time:
    - Apple = m_n_ana
    - Orange = n_ra_ja
    - To eat = c_ _er
    - To drink = b_b_r
  - Finally we have no cues for the target word:
    - Apple =
    - Orange =
    - To eat =
    - To drink =
  - It's likely you'll need to use more pairs in practice. In an experiment, the researchers used 12.[53]
  - Moderate the difficulty by changing the number of pairs or randomising the order in which they are presented (having the same order could act as a cue).
- **Primary phonics**: After teaching students two different graphemes that make the same sound, display the words and get students to make the sounds:
  - "Ou" and "ow" in sound and cow.
  - "Ay" and "ai" in tray and snail.

31

- **Primary maths:**

  - Ask students quick-fire questions to practice number bonds; they can use their whiteboards to respond – e.g. "Give me two numbers that make 5."

  - Set up a do-now task using questions like "How can we make 5?"

  - Ask students to use physical manipulatives (such as Dienes or Numicon) to recreate given numbers. The shapes within Numicon can act as cues for students, as only the correct number of units will fit for a given number.

We must also ensure we provide timely, helpful feedback (see the limitations section on page 33) and adjust the difficulty by including cues where necessary. If students don't have anything to retrieve, they won't reap the benefits of retrieval practice!

Classroom example

Secondary modern foreign languages, by Kirstie Dixon, assistant principal and MFL teacher

Having been introduced to some of the research around retrieval and how it can help students to retain knowledge for longer and access it more easily, I wanted to try to introduce this in my own classroom. My initial quizzes were simply opportunities for me to ask questions about previously covered content and frequently focused on single vocabulary items that were unrelated to each other or the upcoming lesson content. They were not designed with any level of challenge in mind and students were able to use their notes to help them if they were struggling.

Having delved deeper into the research around retrieval and its benefits, I realised that this could be an opportunity to focus regularly on some of the core knowledge that students needed to consolidate. First, I made sure every quiz had a question about one or more of the "big four verbs", as we call them at my school: *avoir* – to have; *être* – to be; *aller* – to go; *faire* – to do. I made this decision as these verbs were part of our core knowledge and, despite asking students to learn them, I found myself regularly needing to reteach them. In these initial quizzes my question forms were generally unchanged, usually focusing on stems such as "What does X mean?" or "How do we say Y?" I wanted students to be able to recognise and produce this core vocabulary, so I ensured the questions required students to translate both from and into French.

As I continued to refine my quizzes by reading more about retrieval practice, I realised that I needed to ensure students were only able to use their notes as a very last resort, so I stopped making these available to students to make the retrieval more effortful. My quizzes started to take longer to plan as I tried to make sure there was an appropriate level of difficulty. Sharing this information with students has been an important part of the work I've done to make my quizzes as effective as possible. Teaching them that these are low-stakes quizzes that help them to consolidate their knowledge and show them – and me – where there are gaps has meant students are happy to have a go at each question.

Feedback from students suggests they now feel more confident to attempt these more challenging questions, as they expect to have to "rummage around in their memory" to retrieve the knowledge. They now understand that knowing the answer is in their heads but they can't quite access it yet is an important part of their learning it. As a teacher, it's been encouraging to see even my reluctant language learners, and those who may be less confident or low prior-attaining students, always willing to have a go at quizzes. It's been even better to see those same students grow in confidence as they start to see that they know more.

What are the limitations to be mindful of?

In general, practice testing is very robust and almost always more beneficial for learning than the strategies mentioned in Dunlosky's "much promise" or "less useful" categories. However, Dunlosky and his colleagues point out that the effectiveness of practice testing can depend on corrective feedback being given to students who answer incorrectly.[54] Providing corrective feedback also manages the risk of students being caught out by misconceptions in multiple-choice tests.[55]

At the very least, feedback should tell the student if they are right or wrong, and where necessary should inform students of the correct answer and/or how to get to it. This can range from a nudge, to telling students to check their answers, to revealing the answer on the board, to a fully explained solution. Feedback doesn't mean written feedback for individuals or groups of students, or using general statements like "You need to work on multiplication". Thinking hard about likely errors beforehand will make the feedback process easier.

If students find retrieval too easy – for example, they are quizzed about the different parts of plants at the end of a lesson on plants – they may not reap the rewards,[56] so they may benefit from some forgetting before being tested.

According to the Bjorks, "certain conditions that produce forgetting … actually create opportunities to enhance our level of learning",[57] something we'll unpack further in the next strategy. Conversely, if difficulty is too high and students aren't able to retrieve information successfully (retrieval strength is too low) then some reteaching/restudying may be beneficial before you return to testing. The reteaching/restudying provides an initial boost in storage and retrieval strength[58] that can be further enhanced with testing.

There are other reasons why test difficulty needs to be moderated:

- Too easy and we run the risk of conflating easily retrievable information with well-stored information; students may believe there's no need to test themselves again in future.

- Too hard and we risk demotivating students and putting them off future attempts.

Figuring out the optimal difficulty is no easy task. There's no quick formula or one-size-fits-all solution. It relies on your knowledge of your students and subject, along with your ability to plan for contingencies and adjust appropriately along the way. We also need to differentiate between when something is *easily retrievable* and when it's *learned*, being mindful of the results of the experiment discussed at the start of this section, in which the STTT group achieved the best performance over time.

Takeaways: practice testing

- What:

  □ The fewer the cues, the bigger the benefits.

  □ Testing must be low or no stakes.

  □ Students should test until they can recall each item correctly at least once.

- Why:

  □ Testing involves retrieving information from LTM.

  □ Information retrieved becomes more retrievable in the future.

- How:

  □ Any activity that involves students retrieving target knowledge.

  □ Cues can be added or removed to moderate the level of difficulty.

  □ Must involve corrective feedback.

Distributed practice

Massed:

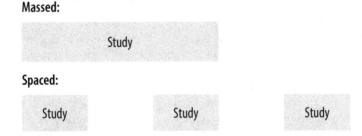

Study

Spaced:

Study   Study   Study

'When playing video games, students see their abilities and skills improve dramatically over time in large part because they keep coming back to play the game in a distributed fashion ... However, for whatever reason, students don't typically use distributed practice as they work toward mastering course content'[59]

What is distributed practice?

In one experiment,[60] students were required to learn 20 French words and their English translations. The students were split into two groups: one group was given 30 minutes to study in one go (massed practice); the other group was given 10 minutes per day across three consecutive days (spaced practice). After their final study session, the students were given a test to establish their retention, followed by a surprise test one week later. The results are illustrated in figure 5.

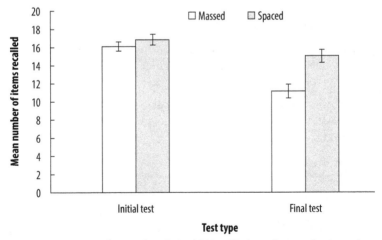

Figure 5. Mean number of items (out of 20) recalled on initial and final tests for massed and spaced groups.[61]

As we can see, there's not much between the two groups after the initial test. However, despite both groups having the *same amount of study time*, the spaced group performed much better on the delayed test.

Distributed (or spaced) practice is the regular repetition of practice over time. It stands in contrast to massed practice, where tasks are clumped together and not regularly repeated (also called blocked practice). For example, over the course of a school term, two students learn about fractions. In school they first learn about adding fractions, then subtracting, then multiplying and lastly dividing, having one lesson on each strategy. After each lesson, student A goes home and practises problems for the strategy learned in that lesson. This practice is massed: all the studying for the strategy is done in quick succession and then not returned to. Student B, meanwhile, goes home and practises problems for the strategy learned in that lesson *and* problems for the strategies covered in the earlier lessons, thereby distributing practice.

Student B could even further distribute their practice by mixing up the problems when they return to the previous strategies (this strays into interleaving, which we'll unpack later in this chapter). As Dunlosky puts it, "The idea is to return to the most important material and concepts repeatedly across class days."[62]

Dunlosky points out that when preparing for exams, students will gain far more from regular practice than from trying to "cram", even when the time spent is equal.[63] This is incredibly useful to know for teachers and students alike: studying for two hours over a week can be far more effective than studying for two hours the evening before the exam.

Why does distributed practice work?

'Certain conditions that produce forgetting ... also enhance the learning of that information when it is restudied'[64]

Dunlosky and his colleagues note that many theories have been offered to explain why distributed practice works, and suggest that its effectiveness may be down to a combination of these theories.[65] First, let's look at figure 6.

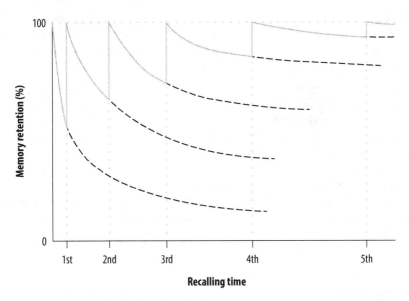

Figure 6. Forgetting curve with the effects of spacing.[66]

This graph is adapted from the Ebbinghaus forgetting curve that we discussed in chapter 1 (see page 22); the dashed lines show the rate of forgetting if recall doesn't take place. What this graph shows is how distributing practice can mitigate the effects of forgetting. Does this mean we should keep going over information so we don't forget it? The answer is: almost definitely not. In fact, if we really want to remember new information, "the best approach might be to allow ourselves to forget it first".[67]

This idea is demonstrated nicely by the experiment we discussed earlier. Each group spent an equal amount of time on the task, but the spaced group had time to forget some of the information before relearning it. After the initial session, their retrieval strength would have dropped rapidly. But, crucially, lower retrieval strengths allow for *bigger gains* in storage strength.[68] So, when the spaced group restudied, they were able to retain the information for longer because their storage strength was higher. This also explains why, despite equal time spent on the task, the massed group didn't perform as well: because they studied continuously their retrieval strength remained high, meaning their gains in storage strength were smaller than for the spaced group.

To generalise these findings, the more difficult it is to retrieve information, the bigger the gains in storage and retrieval strength.[69] These gains mean we retain the target information for longer, can recall it more easily and can relearn it quicker, because we need fewer cues for successful retrieval. Dunlosky and his colleagues draw parallels with the mechanisms behind practice testing: a second study session acts as a reminder and memories from the first session are retrieved.[70]

When practice is massed it *feels* easier: the success rate is often high and so students tend to lean on this strategy. Massed practice also lulls us into a false sense of security: the high success rate leads teachers and students to believe the target material has been "learned", when in fact we haven't achieved the *permanent* change in knowledge by which we define learning. Distributed practice, by contrast, is much harder. We're working with information that is not so fresh in our memories, so our initial success rate drops. But, as many studies quoted by Willingham[71] and Dunlosky[72] show, this decrease in initial success (versus massed practice) tends to be followed by a significant increase in success when there's a delay between study and test.

How can we use distributed practice in the classroom?

Distributed practice lends itself nicely to practice testing; the two are often used in conjunction with each other and a lot of the examples below incorporate practice testing, so don't be surprised to find some overlap.

- Use starters to review previous learning.[73]

- Use daily/weekly retrieval activities that include material covered in previous lessons.

- Set practice tests that are cumulative (new topics are added alongside older ones) rather than modular (focusing only on the most recent topics).[74]

- Have "summative assessments that are shorter and more frequent rather than longer and less frequent".[75]

- Modify schemes of work to see topics across a year and plan regular opportunities to revisit older items.

- Sit down as a department and think about the core "things" you want students to know/be able to do by the end of the year (e.g. specific maths equations). Give students regular quizzes that incorporate these topics.

- Break larger topics into smaller pieces that can be practised more easily through quizzing or homework.

- Where students need to learn key vocabulary throughout a course, set quizzes that test recently learned and older vocabulary. You could:

  □ Ask students to give three key terms from last week and three from last term, plus their definitions.

- ◻ To reduce the difficulty, you could provide the keywords and ask students for the definitions, or vice versa.

- Set homework involving questions from previously covered topics:

  - ◻ Homework that only covers an older topic.

  - ◻ Homework on a recently covered topic that includes questions from older topics.

  - ◻ Topics are regularly mixed to ensure broad coverage and no single topic is over-repeated.

- Help students to plan their studying:

  - ◻ Support them to create a "study planner" to schedule regular reviews; a few hours spread over a week are likely to be more productive than a block of hours in one day.

  - ◻ Remind students of key concepts you've already covered in class that they can revisit themselves.

  - ◻ Explain to students the pitfalls of "cramming" for a test vs regular revision; regular revision may even mean they end up spending less total time studying for tests.[76]

- **English**: After using practice testing to help students recall the key quotes from *Macbeth*, reuse the tests at intervals throughout the year to ensure the retention prevails over a longer term.

- **Science**:

  - ◻ Reuse some of the diagrams/equations from our practice testing (see page 30) at spaced intervals within starter activities or homework.

  - ◻ After finishing a topic, use an activity that covers knowledge from the whole topic. Students will have to retrieve older as well as more recent knowledge, so this activity will inherently include some spacing.

    - ■ Try a blank-sheet retrieval task – e.g. "Write down everything you know about photosynthesis."

- **Maths**: After teaching students to find the area of various different 2D shapes over a period of lessons, give them a review activity with questions on all the shapes covered, not just the most recent ones.

- **Music**: Reuse short quizzes on key technical knowledge like:

  - ◻ What is the pattern of semi-tones for a major chord?

  - ◻ What is the pattern of semi-tones for a minor chord?

◻ What notes would you play for a triad of C major?

- **Primary maths**: Knowing that 2 + 8 = 10 will make it easier to learn that 12 + 8 = 20 or 20 + 80 = 100. As such, regular opportunities to revisit these more simple number bonds will facilitate addition with larger numbers.

- **Primary geography**: The different countries around the world and cities within the UK are key bits of knowledge in primary. To aid consolidation, make sure students are repeatedly exposed to these facts across the entire phase through weekly, monthly and termly recap.

Classroom example

Primary literacy, by Jessica Appleton, key stage 1 class teacher

After looking at the research on distributed practice, I thought it seemed a useful strategy for helping my pupils to improve their fluency and retain information in the long term. A strategy that I thought would work well with my practice was using low-stakes quizzing to re-expose students to key content. Having read through the research, I had some questions about implementing spacing and quizzing with younger children, including what the optimum spacing between revisiting material should be. This was something I was mindful of during implementation (as the most important aspect of quizzing is that it's happening at all).

I decided to take advantage of "downtime" by using transitions to quiz students on already taught material. I didn't have a methodical way of exposing my pupils to the first 100 high-frequency words (the most common words in the English language), so my plan was to introduce a different word at the beginning of each phonics lesson and then use "transition quizzes" to re-expose the children to those words.

When implementing the quizzes, there were some key factors to consider to ensure their effectiveness. The first was consistency: making sure the quizzes happened every day could have been difficult with an already squeezed timetable. However, using transition times and keeping the sessions short (five minutes maximum) made this more achievable.

The second consideration was balancing difficulty and success. The quizzes needed to be challenging enough for the pupils to find retrieval of the knowledge effortful, but not so difficult that they struggled to recall anything at all. This was something I grappled with initially. However, completing regular mini-assessments of high-frequency words with key children in the class helped to fine-tune the process.

Finally, I needed to support the wide range of abilities in the class, so every child was challenged appropriately. I colour-coded my flashcards based on whether words were phonically plausible (green) or not (red) for pupils who needed more support. The colour-coding supported pupils by helping them to identify whether a word was phonetically decodable or not (e.g. there and their). Meanwhile, I introduced a spelling element to challenge stronger readers: during quizzing sessions I would call out a word and ask children to orally spell it back to me. This had the added benefit of giving them practice in using the letter names rather than the sounds.

Although there were some teething problems, these transition quizzes have now become part of the everyday routine, giving pupils daily distributed practice in retrieving high-frequency words. This has allowed me to reflect and adapt the quizzes each time to include previously misspelt words. As practice aids knowledge retention, the children should build up their knowledge of these words rapidly. I use my pupil knowledge and assessments of the children to constantly revise and plan which words need to be covered next in order for the quizzes to be relevant and challenging. My regular assessments show improvements in children's ability to read these words. Meanwhile, it would seem that my pupils are starting to translate this knowledge into their reading: during reading sessions their recognition of these words is also improving.

What are the limitations to be mindful of?

The evidence base for distributed practice is incredibly robust and the strategy has been shown to work in both laboratory and classroom settings, as well as across a wide range of tasks and subjects.[77] However, there are still a few things to be mindful of during implementation:

- Textbooks/course materials don't tend to lend themselves to distributed practice,[78] so teachers/students may have to make their own materials.
- Dunlosky points out that students don't tend to engage in distributed practice without external prompting factors.[79] In fact, their time spent on studying peaks closest to an exam. As such, students may need training in how to implement distributed practice effectively.
- Linked to this, students will always prioritise the most immediate exam, so speaking to colleagues about when exams are taking place will allow for adequate study time.

- It's important to differentiate between distributed practice and *review*.[80] Students must be able to achieve some success with distributed practice. If their memories are too fragile, students should have a chance to *review* the material by restudying it or being presented with it again.

- The impact on learning depends on *how* students use their time with distributed practice. For example, continuously rereading information in a distributed manner is highly unlikely to aid learning as this isn't guaranteed to be an effortful process.

- Figuring out an optimal gap is a significant challenge. Although it's critical that there is some gap (so we can harness the impact of forgetting), the optimal gap for any individual student will likely be impacted by factors such as their existing prior knowledge, the amount of attention they paid during initial instruction and their initial success rate. However, one study suggests that a gap that's "too long" is better than one that's "too short".[81]

Takeaways: distributed practice

- **What:**

  ▫ Regularly return to important concepts.

  ▫ Mix previously covered material with newer material.

- **Why:**

  ▫ Forgetting is inevitable, but knowing this allows us to plan accordingly.

  ▫ Some forgetting must occur in order to reap the benefits of distributed practice.

- **How:**

  ▫ Any activity that involves students having to think hard about knowledge that's already been covered.

  ▫ Can be combined very effectively with retrieval practice.

  ▫ It's not enough for distributed practice to be left to students to make use of – we must also make use of it in our classrooms.

Part 2: Strategies with much promise

Interleaving

Massed:

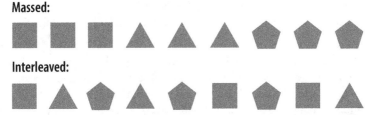

Interleaved:

'Interleaving … helps the learner to choose the correct strategy to solve a problem and helps them see the links, similarities, and differences'[82]

What is interleaving?

In one experiment, students were taught different formulas relating to the properties of prisms (number of faces, corners, edges or angles).[83] The students were placed into one of two groups: the blocked group (massed practice) worked on problems involving one type of property before moving on to the next type, while the interleaved group worked on all four properties at once in a random order. The number of problems was equal for each group. After the study sessions, both groups of students were given an initial test, followed by a final test one day later. The results are illustrated in figure 7.

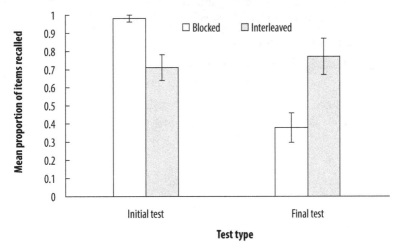

Figure 7. Mean proportion of items recalled on initial and final tests for blocked and interleaved practice groups.[84]

Although the blocked group significantly outperformed the interleaved group on the initial test, their performance declined dramatically over just one day, while the mean performance of the interleaved group stayed high. Furthermore, analysis of the final test revealed that the blocked group made more than four times as many errors owing to incorrect identification of the problem.

Put simply, interleaving is the mixing up of related problems.[85] An inherent level of spacing occurs with interleaving, because by mixing up problems you're creating space between them. However, there are several nuances when it comes to interleaving and how it should be used effectively: simply jumbling up random problems and putting them together, or rearranging schemes of work to become mix-and-match topics, isn't what the research suggests. The problems must be selected so that students are forced to discriminate between related concepts; not just apply a method but first choose the *correct* method.[86] This is what distinguishes interleaving from spaced practice. For a concrete example, you may wish to skip ahead to the classroom example on page 47 before returning to this section.

Interleaving is hard: students have to think about which method they need to use as well as actually using it. Massed practice is easier and students often find their performance improves much more quickly compared with interleaved practice; however, as shown by the experiment discussed earlier, these gains are short-lived.[87] Crucially, although interleaving can impair short-term performance, it's been demonstrated to improve delayed performance, relative to massed practice, and to improve students' ability to discriminate between appropriate methods during delayed performance.[88]

Why does interleaving work?

'Interleaving is thought to assist the drawing of comparisons between related but discrete items of learning'[89]

Interleaving inherently involves a degree of distributed practice, which, as we've already seen, is supported by robust evidence for its effectiveness. But is there a quality specific to interleaving that can make it even more effective than spaced practice?

One suggestion is that interleaving aids learning by forcing students to discern between the different methods that could be used to solve the problems.[90] In doing so, students attend to the key features of and between related problems, making it more likely that they'll recognise these features when they are next exposed to them.[91] This theory is supported by the findings of the experiment discussed in the previous section: errors made as a result of misattributing formulas were 36% lower for the interleaved group than the blocked group.[92] Another experiment designed to test "time on task" as a factor found that learners' results were best in the interleaved condition, suggesting it was the requirement to discern and identify that aided learning.[93]

Another suggestion uses the theory behind retrieval. Students working through similar problems in a massed manner will likely only need to retrieve the correct method once before executing it several times. In an interleaved problem set, however, students need to constantly retrieve the correct method before executing it, multiplying the opportunities for retrieval.[94]

There may be an overlap between all these explanations: the opportunities for retrieval would be tied to the contextual cues (the features of the problems),[95] strengthening the relationship between the cue and the action, so future exposure to those cues would be more likely to result in the correct action.

How can we use interleaving in the classroom?

- Although we've previously compared interleaving to distributed practice, it's important not to see them as separate. You can combine the two strategies by giving students a set of related mixed problems at the end of a week/term/topic. Students will experience a gap after the initial learning (distributed practice) and will work through a set of randomly mixed but related problems (interleaving).

- Adapt textbook exercises (which tend to be massed) so they can be interleaved – for example, by using screenshots of e-textbooks to mix up problems where they have been massed.

- Starters/do-now tasks could comprise interleaved problems on previously covered topics.

- When setting up schemes of work, plan opportunities where interleaving might be helpful – e.g. placing plant and animal cell lessons together, or grouping different artists and their styles together.

- When introducing new concepts that are similar to old ones, explicitly talk about the similarities and differences so students know what to look for when attempting interleaved practice.

- Vary when interleaving is introduced: it may be helpful to start off with massed practice, allowing students to develop a level of fluency with individual strategies first.

- Think about where you want to draw students' attention to similarities and differences in techniques:

▫ **Art**: You might put different artists and their styles together.[96]

▫ **PE**: You could mix up the different types of techniques within a skill, such as cricket strokes or baseball pitches. When teaching shooting or throwing techniques, you could vary the distances and directions that the shot/throw is made from.[97]

▫ **Music**: One experiment used interleaved practice with secondary school clarinet students:[98]

- Students were given three short pieces of music to play.

- The massed group practised one piece per day, while the interleaved group spent all three days practising all three pieces.

- The number of practice opportunities for each piece was equal for each group.

- Researchers found that at the end of each day the massed group was able to play faster than the interleaved group, but after a 24-hour delay the interleaved group was significantly faster.

• **Primary English**: This idea is particularly helpful when revising different sounds. For example, mixing up similar sounding words that are spelled differently, such as "cow" or "bow", could help students to distinguish the similarities and differences.

▫ Sound out each word and get students to write it down.

▫ Provide corrective feedback for students where needed.

• **Primary maths**:

- When familiarising students with different types of manipulatives (e.g. Dienes and Numicon), interleave these activities to get students thinking hard about the differences.

- Vary the ways in which students to learn to read the time. For example, vary the size/shape of the clock faces, or alternate practice between reading the time and having to draw clock faces for a given time.

Classroom example

Secondary maths – an example from my own practice

Having explored the research on interleaving and how consistently it was found to help in maths, I was keen to try it in my classroom. I looked at a few topics and settled on trialling interleaving while teaching students how to use the different mathematical operations with fractions. I had searched some textbooks and found that most exercises looked like this:

$$1. a) \frac{1}{4} + \frac{1}{5} \quad b) \frac{1}{4} + \frac{1}{8} \quad c) \frac{1}{8} + \frac{1}{5} \quad d) \frac{1}{8} + \frac{1}{7}$$

$$2. a) \frac{1}{4} - \frac{1}{5} \quad b) \frac{1}{4} - \frac{1}{8} \quad c) \frac{1}{8} - \frac{1}{5} \quad d) \frac{1}{8} - \frac{1}{7}$$

$$3. a) \frac{1}{4} \times \frac{1}{5} \quad b) \frac{1}{4} \times \frac{1}{8} \quad c) \frac{1}{8} \times \frac{1}{5} \quad d) \frac{1}{8} \times \frac{1}{7}$$

$$4. a) \frac{1}{4} \div \frac{1}{5} \quad b) \frac{1}{4} \div \frac{1}{8} \quad c) \frac{1}{8} \div \frac{1}{5} \quad d) \frac{1}{8} \div \frac{1}{7}$$

Example 1: massed practice.

Here the questions are massed by operation. It's likely that the student would have to think hard for questions a and b, but would then spot the pattern and re-engage the process without thinking too hard. To incorporate the "mixing" aspect of interleaving, I changed the order of the fractions without changing the actual questions themselves:

$$1. a) \frac{1}{4} + \frac{1}{5} \quad b) \frac{1}{4} - \frac{1}{5} \quad c) \frac{1}{4} \times \frac{1}{5} \quad d) \frac{1}{4} \div \frac{1}{5}$$

$$2. a) \frac{1}{4} + \frac{1}{8} \quad b) \frac{1}{4} - \frac{1}{8} \quad c) \frac{1}{4} \times \frac{1}{8} \quad d) \frac{1}{4} \div \frac{1}{8}$$

$$3. a) \frac{1}{8} + \frac{1}{5} \quad b) \frac{1}{8} - \frac{1}{5} \quad c) \frac{1}{8} \times \frac{1}{5} \quad d) \frac{1}{8} \div \frac{1}{5}$$

$$4. a) \frac{1}{8} + \frac{1}{7} \quad b) \frac{1}{8} - \frac{1}{7} \quad c) \frac{1}{8} \times \frac{1}{7} \quad d) \frac{1}{8} \div \frac{1}{7}$$

Example 2: mixed practice.

After mixing up the problems, some natural spacing has occurred: the addition problems are now separated by three problems of a different type. Despite this, I was concerned that students would spot the pattern and then repeat the processes without noticing the key differences, so I made another small change to help me come to a final version:

$$1.\, a)\ \frac{1}{4} + \frac{1}{5}\ \ b)\ \frac{1}{4} - \frac{1}{5}\ \ c)\ \frac{1}{4} \times \frac{1}{5}\ \ d)\ \frac{1}{4} \div \frac{1}{5}$$

$$2.\, a)\ \frac{1}{4} - \frac{1}{8}\ \ b)\ \frac{1}{4} \times \frac{1}{8}\ \ c)\ \frac{1}{4} \div \frac{1}{8}\ \ d)\ \frac{1}{4} + \frac{1}{8}$$

$$3.\, a)\ \frac{1}{8} \div \frac{1}{5}\ \ b)\ \frac{1}{8} - \frac{1}{5}\ \ c)\ \frac{1}{8} + \frac{1}{5}\ \ d)\ \frac{1}{8} \times \frac{1}{5}$$

$$4.\, a)\ \frac{1}{8} \times \frac{1}{7}\ \ b)\ \frac{1}{8} \div \frac{1}{7}\ \ c)\ \frac{1}{8} - \frac{1}{7}\ \ d)\ \frac{1}{8} + \frac{1}{7}$$

Example 3: interleaved practice.

In example 2 the problems are mixed but still follow a pattern, whereas in example 3 the problems are randomly mixed. Part of the power of interleaving lies in students being forced to discern and select between different methods. Therefore, my thinking was that example 3 would require students to select which method to choose *and* execute that method for *each individual problem*. After implementation in class, there was an increase in time on task (and sometimes frustration!) when students used the interleaved problems compared with the massed problems; it was clear students were having to think much harder with the interleaved problems. It was also interesting to see that when they made errors in the later end-of-term test, these tended to be calculation errors (e.g. wrong numbers) rather than incorrect technique errors, indicating that the students had likely correctly matched the technique to the operation.

However, this is a fine art and finding the right time to introduce interleaving hasn't always been easy – I have got it wrong at times! In these circumstances, textbook exercises have proven useful, giving students an opportunity to do some massed practice (with feedback) to develop fluency before they embark on interleaved practice.

What are the limitations to be mindful of?

We must decide exactly what we're asking students to attend to before introducing interleaving. In the fractions example, my goal was for students to discern how different operations should be carried out. It would be a poor exercise if the goal was for students to understand the importance of lowest common denominator when adding fractions. Before presenting students with problems we should work backwards, thinking first about what goal we're trying to achieve.

We also want to bear in mind what we're mixing up. While mixing *within* disciplines can be helpful, mixing *between* disciplines (e.g. interleaving physics problems with questions on English literature) is likely to be confusing for students and even a hindrance to learning. Furthermore, one experiment found that students deemed interleaving a less helpful strategy for their learning and rated it as more challenging,[99] so we should think hard about the impact it may have on student perseverance and motivation.

The benefits of interleaving don't extend to all disciplines:[100]

- A lot of the research showing positive effects has been limited to maths and tasks involving motor skills (music, sport, etc.).[101]
- Positive effects have been shown in engineering, some aspects of medical studies and studies involving learning artists' painting styles.[102]
- When interleaving was tested in MFL and in studying English grammar rules, no effect was found.[103]
- Textbooks/course materials don't tend to lend themselves to interleaved practice, so teachers/students may have to make their own materials.

Takeaways: interleaving

- **What**:
  - The mixing up of related concepts/problems in order to discern similarities and differences.
  - Mixing previously covered material with newer material, if related.

- **Why:**

  - The mixing up forces students to select *and* execute an appropriate method.
  - The selection provides additional opportunities for retrieval compared with massed practice.

- **How:**

  - Draw attention to the key differences/similarities during explanations and examples.
  - Work backwards, starting with the goal of the task and then selecting the problems.
  - Ensure there's no discernible pattern to the order of questions.

Elaborative interrogation and self-explanation

Currently it says $y - 4 = x$. To make y the subject, I need to get it by itself, so I need to move the 4 to the other side. Because the 4 is being subtracted, I need to do the inverse and add it, so it will become $y = x + 4$.

'Students should have little trouble using elaborative interrogation, because it simply involves encouraging them to ask the question "why?" when they are studying'[104]

What are elaborative interrogation and self-explanation?

To explain these two ideas, Dunlosky gives us the example of a student studying the process of photosynthesis:

> "*Imagine a student reading an introductory passage on photosynthesis: 'It is a process in which a plant converts carbon dioxide and water into sugar, which is its food. The process gives off oxygen.' If the student were using elaborative interrogation while reading, she would try to explain why this fact is true ... If the student were using self-explanation, then she would try to explain how this new information is related to information that she already knows.*"[105]

As you can discern from Dunlosky's example, there's a significant overlap between the two strategies. For example, it would be difficult to explain why this fact is true without using any information you already know (e.g. that sugar is a type of food) and difficult to add in new information without assisting in establishing the truth of the statement (e.g. if the student knows that humans breathe in oxygen and breathe out carbon dioxide, she can draw parallels with the new information she's read). We could make a rough distinction by saying that elaborative interrogation leans towards answering *why* something happens or is the way it is, while self-explanations lean towards answering *how* something happens or *what* is happening.

One strategy is called "principle-based self-explanations". These self-explanations relate a step in a worked solution (e.g. in a maths problem) or the feature of an object (e.g. the appearance of an animal) to an underlying principle (e.g. BIDMAS or evolutionary traits).[106] For example, in seeking to explain why 2 x 3 = 6, we might refer to the idea that multiplication can be thought of as how many "lots" of a particular item I have: in this case, 2 "lots" of 3 will give me 6. Our goal is to connect specific situations to more general principles.[107]

However, as this book is about implementing effective strategies in the classroom, distinguishing between elaborative interrogation and self-explanation is likely less important than simply being able to implement their key features. So, we'll focus more broadly on what the mechanisms are, why they work and how we might make use of them in the classroom.

Why do elaborative interrogation and self-explanation work?

'Trying to elaborate on why a fact may be true, even when the explanations are not entirely on the mark, can still benefit understanding and retention'[108]

It's likely that a few different mechanisms are at play that can make these strategies effective. One mechanism relates to the effort required: explaining or expanding on an idea or process is effortful and demands active processing of the idea or process at hand.[109] In doing so, students are likely to draw on prior knowledge, which leads us to our second mechanism: integration with prior knowledge.[110] Integration with prior knowledge inherently involves having to retrieve knowledge – a strategy we know is helpful – so during integration we're likely also consolidating that prior knowledge. Furthermore, it's likely that the successful integration of new knowledge will make the existing knowledge easier to recall later on,[111] because we're adding new routes to already well-etched parts of our LTM, rather than random routes in isolation.

Another potential mechanism relates to interleaving: elaborative interrogation and self-explanation involve processing similarities and differences between related ideas.[112] For example, explaining or elaborating on why something might be true in one case (e.g. finding a common denominator when adding fractions) but not in another (e.g. not finding a common denominator when multiplying fractions) can aid the organisation of the new information, ensuring it's integrated with the appropriate prior knowledge.

Students who use these strategies tend to be more successful in problems that involve transfer,[113] i.e. problems where students need to use existing knowledge and apply it in unfamiliar contexts. This could be because in making connections to general principles, students are consistently examining the deep structures of the material, making it more likely that they'll recognise those same structures in future even when the context has changed.

How can we use elaborative interrogation and self-explanation in the classroom?

These techniques are already often used effectively by teachers and it's worth thinking about how we can get our students using them too. Elaborative interrogation and self-explanation are most helpful when new knowledge needs to be connected to existing knowledge, or when abstract ideas and general principles need to be applied to a specific context.

- Questioning can be an incredibly effective way of incorporating these two strategies into lessons:

  ◦ Help students to tie particular situations to general principles by asking why something is *always* true or will *always* work.[114]

  ◦ With the aim of making *why?* a regular facet of our teaching, ask students to explain a situation using information beyond that presented to them in the moment.

- After giving multiple reasons why something is true, students can explain which is best and justify their answer:

  Which best explains why angles in a square add up to 360° and why?

  a. Because there are four right angles, each of 90°.

  b. Because we can split the square into two triangles, and we know angles in a triangle add up to 180°.

- The use of non-examples:

  □ A non-example is one that's intentionally incorrect – this may be a mistake in the steps to the solution or in the solution itself.

  □ After showing a non-example, ask students to come up with an explanation of why it's wrong.

- When teaching processes, get students to explain to themselves what's happening during each step:

  □ Model the process to students by first explaining the steps involved, thinking aloud and making explicit connections to previously covered knowledge.

  □ When the students go on to follow the process, encourage them to explain the steps to themselves in the same way.

- Provide specific prompts when displaying problems to students:

  □ **Maths**: Rather than just stating the fact that pi is an irrational number, ask students to explain why this is the case. Push for further examples or non-examples in order to add more connections to this central idea.

  □ **Science**: Start with a question such as, "If we place an ice cube on the tabletop, what will happen?" Students will likely respond, "It will melt." Then ask them why, prompting them to think about heat exchange.[115]

  □ **History**: After teaching students about both world wars, set them tasks such as:[116]

    ▪ Give three key differences between the two world wars.

    ▪ List as many reasons as you can for why each world war started.

  □ **English**: Display a factual statement like "The witches plan to meet Macbeth after the battle". Ask students "Why might the witches plan to meet Macbeth?" or take it further and ask "Why might the witches plan to meet Macbeth after, rather than before, the battle?" This will prompt more elaboration than simply asking "When do the witches plan to meet Macbeth?"[117]

◻ **Geography**: When teaching students about the Thar desert case study:

- Preemptively get students to connect prior learning about general principles to this specific case study by asking them to name some issues that make it hard to live or work in a desert.

- After telling students that many people who live in the Thar desert are subsistence farmers, ask them to think about why this might be the case. This prompts students to connect the case study to more general ideas about the challenges of living in a desert.

◻ **Primary maths**: Ask students to justify their answers with some examples of the thinking that we're trying to prompt:

- Teacher: "How can you prove that $8 + 2 = 10$?"

  Student response/thinking: "I know $8 + 2 = 10$ because the Numicons match."

- Teacher: "Explain how you know that $10 + 2 = 12$."

  Student response/thinking: "I put 10 in my head and then I counted on 2."

◻ **Primary English**: Prompt students to think about how positioning affects spellings:

- Teacher: "How do you spell the word 'happy'? Why isn't it spelled 'happee'?"

- Student response/thinking: "I know it's 'happy' because the 'ee' sound at the end of a word is normally spelled 'y' rather than 'ee'."

◻ **Primary science**: After teaching students about evergreen trees, ask them to characterise a tree they are unfamiliar with and justify their answer:

- Student response/thinking: "I know this tree is evergreen because it's winter and the tree still has green leaves."

What are the limitations to be mindful of?

Elaborative interrogation and self-explanation can be fairly straightforward to implement in the classroom, requiring little training. However, prior knowledge is a key factor in how much benefit students gain from these strategies. The benefits are greater when elaborations are more precise, when student prior knowledge is higher and when elaborations are self-generated rather than provided.[118] In addition, if students lack the relevant knowledge then they won't benefit,[119] because they can't elaborate on something they don't know. We may need to check students have an appropriate level of prior knowledge before using this strategy.

We must also be careful that students are *adding information* to what's present in front of them,[120] rather than just summarising or paraphrasing the material. Lastly, it's critical to ensure students give themselves the *correct* self-explanations, so teachers need to find ways to check students' thinking and share the correct knowledge.

Takeaways: elaborative interrogation and self-explanation

- **What**:

  - Using additional knowledge to make connections between particular situations and general principles.

  - Explaining the why, what or how of a process or idea.

- **Why**:

  - Connecting new knowledge to existing knowledge makes it easier to retrieve.

  - The connection process allows new and existing knowledge to be organised effectively.

- **How**:

  - Get students to make connections between new material and prior knowledge.

  - Probe their thinking to allow extra information to be added to thinking about new material.

Part 3: Less useful strategies

> Lorem ipsum lorem
> ipsum lorem ipsum
> Lorem ipsum lorem
> ipsum lorem ipsum
> Lorem ipsum lorem
> ipsum lorem ipsum
> Lorem ipsum lorem
> ipsum lorem ipsum
> Lorem ipsum lorem
> ipsum lorem ipsum

In this part, rather than looking at examples of classroom practice for the strategies in question, we'll instead delve deeper into why these strategies have been categorised as "less useful". Dunlosky has characterised the strategies as less effective not because they are in and of themselves "bad", but because they are generally *not as good* as the strategies we've already considered.

There's an opportunity cost with all strategies: time spent using one strategy could instead be spent on a different, more effective strategy. This idea is crucial to unlocking Dunlosky's paper; according to Dylan Wiliam, "opportunity cost is the single most [important] concept in educational improvement".[121] As such, teachers should think carefully about when to use the following strategies, what their goal is in using them, and whether that goal might be better served by the other strategies we've covered in this chapter. It's also worth noting that students tend to favour the following strategies,[122] so teachers may want to think hard about how to help students select the most appropriate strategy and how to help them move away from less appropriate ones.

Summarisation

> 'Summarization involves paraphrasing the most important ideas within a text'[123]

What is summarisation?

Many of us have used summarisation: it may have helped us to organise our thinking, pick out key points or create a permanent record of an oral presentation. However, our use of summarisation will likely have been very variable, with more/fewer diagrams, words and equations depending on the subject matter. Herein lies the first barrier: it's difficult to pin down exactly what summarising is. The strategy could involve summarising material into a few words, a sentence, a paragraph; the source material could be an essay, a book, a diagram; it may be from a written or an oral presentation. For now, let's be as general as possible and go with the following definition of summarisation: any activity with the purpose of recording key information and rephrasing it.[124] Through such an activity, we make a decision about what the core information is and then organise it in a way that's helpful to us.

Under what conditions might summarisation work?

One claim is that summarisation can boost learning as it involves paying attention to the key parts of the subject and, in doing so, extracting higher-level meaning.[125] When summarising, we're required to make connections within the subject matter as well as between the subject matter and our existing knowledge. This is helpful for two reasons: connecting new ideas to existing ideas can aid the building of knowledge and actively help the learning process;[126] it also involves the retrieval of existing knowledge, which, as we've seen, can be an extremely effective way of consolidating knowledge. Furthermore, paraphrasing the important points from the subject matter involves a more active processing of the material than simply selecting the key points or copying out verbatim.[127]

Why is summarisation a less useful strategy?

This is, for me, the most controversial of Dunlosky's categorisations. Fiorella and Mayer include summarisation as one of their eight generative learning strategies,[128] while Kirschner, Neelen, Hoof and Surma have also written about how it can be used effectively.[129] So why does Dunlosky describe this as a "less useful" strategy?

There are a few reasons for this categorisation. First, the strategy appears to be helpful only to people already skilled in effective summarisation.[130] So, in order for all students to benefit from the strategy, we would need to spend time training students to become effective summarisers – time that could be spent using another strategy. An additional consideration is our context: training university students in effective summarisation would be a very different matter from training primary school students.

Second, the benefits of summarisation appear limited to materials that are already in a summarisation-friendly form: essays, stories or other text-based materials. Subjects such as maths or physics aren't likely to see the same benefits, owing to their more spatial nature.[131] The nature of summarisation will also vary from subject to subject, so it's quite plausible that a person skilled at summarising in one context may struggle to summarise in another context, as summarisation is not necessarily a generalisable skill.[132] Finally, we can only pick out key knowledge if we have prior knowledge that allows us to figure out which knowledge is key in the first place.

So, although the evidence suggests that summarisation *can* be useful, we have to ask ourselves: is summarisation *more* useful than the other strategies discussed in this book?

Highlighting and rereading

'[Highlighting and underlining] typically appeal to students because they are simple to use, do not entail training, and do not require students to invest much time beyond what is already required for reading the material'[133]

What are highlighting and rereading?

Highlighting is an almost universally used strategy that involves picking out key bits of information from texts, diagrams or annotations. I'm sure the vast majority of us can relate to the sight of students with brightly coloured notes, textbooks and much more by the time exam season comes around. Rereading is also an incredibly popular strategy, with one study noting that more than 80% of students study by rereading their notes or textbooks.[134] Unlike summarisation, neither of these strategies are likely to require training in order to be used effectively, but do their ease and high level of use equate to a high impact on learning?

Under what conditions might highlighting and rereading work?

Let's return to an idea discussed in chapter 1: there are very few "bad" strategies, but there are many bad uses for any given strategy.

When thinking about the conditions under which highlighting and rereading may be effective, we need to first consider our goal. If our goal is learning then it's difficult to see how these strategies can achieve that in isolation: they are not effortful, so they are unlikely to aid learning. However, if a student wants to be able to select the bits of information from a text/diagram that are most worth revisiting, highlighting can help to focus their study.[135] Simply rereading those highlighted sections is unlikely to help, but combining this strategy with practice testing or flashcards, for example, can aid learning as this is a more effortful process. So, a student could highlight a key quote or equation and then practise retrieving the information, before checking by looking at the section they have already highlighted, which saves them having to sift through extraneous information.

Rereading can be helpful in situations where students find retrieval too difficult or have forgotten the information altogether; as previously discussed, practice testing only works if there's something to be retrieved. In these situations, students may be better off rereading or looking up the key information before going into some practice testing.

One great practical point from Dunlosky is this: "I would not take away highlighters from students; they are a security blanket ... however, students need to know that highlighting is only the beginning of the journey."[136]

Why are highlighting and rereading less useful strategies?

Both are fairly easy processes: Dunlosky notes that it's quite plausible for students to be passively reading or skimming a text and/or highlighting while at the same time thinking about something completely unrelated.[137] As we saw from Daniel Willingham's model of memory in chapter 1, we can only learn what we pay attention to (see page 20). As such, we can read or highlight significant amounts of information without actively processing much of it – it doesn't even enter our WM so it has no chance of being learned.

Highlighting and rereading also have other limitations. For example, although rereading can be of benefit when recall of text is required, it doesn't necessarily enhance students' understanding of the text content and any benefits don't tend to be long-lasting.[138] One study even found that students who highlighted performed worse on tests where they needed to make connections across different ideas within the text.[139]

The biggest variable in all this is the student. As one colleague told me, "When my teacher came to me and asked why I'd highlighted the whole chapter when they only wanted me to highlight the important ideas, I said, 'Because all of it is important!'" If a student lacks the background knowledge or guidance to be able to discern what is and isn't worth focusing on, they'll need to restudy the material and develop that knowledge before going on to narrow their focus.

Keyword mnemonic and imagery for text

'For students who enjoy using imagery and for materials that afford its use, [imagery] likely will not hurt (and may even improve) learning'[140]

What are keyword mnemonic and imagery for text?

Dunlosky places both these strategies under the broader strategy of mental imagery (the development of internal images to expand on what's being studied) but he focuses on these two because they have undergone empirical scrutiny and so are easier to draw conclusions on.[141] For keyword mnemonic, the research focused mainly on its use in learning foreign language vocabulary. For example, a student wanting to learn the French for tooth, *la dent*, may imagine a dentist holding a tooth; if they want to learn the Spanish word for worm, *gusano*, they may imagine a goose holding a worm.[142] The student has found an English word that sounds similar to the foreign word (dentist for *la dent*) and created an image around the English word to remind them of the translation. Although the research worked with English as the "primary" language, it's more than likely the effect could be replicated with any alternative primary language.

Imagery for text involves students creating mental images of the content they are studying. For example, in one study, students were reading about the nature of water molecules, specifically their electromagnetic properties.[143] While reading, students were instructed to mentally imagine the content of each paragraph using simple and clear mental images. The strategy could be applied to other scenarios, such as imagining scientific processes (photosynthesis, blood circulation, etc.) or stories from literature (e.g. imagining a particular scene).

Under what conditions might keyword mnemonic and imagery for text work?

Little training is required to implement these strategies in the classroom and they are unlikely to hinder learning. So, where the materials support their use and where students find them helpful, there may be some small benefit to keyword mnemonic and imagery for text. There's also limited opportunity cost, as students can use these strategies *while* they are studying, rather than when going back over material. The range of materials for which the strategies can be effective is quite broad, including medical terminology and people's names and accomplishments, to name a few.[144] To get the most out of keyword mnemonic and imagery for text, as with highlighting, it would be best to combine them with the strategies mentioned in parts 1 and 2 of this chapter.

In studies, the keywords tended to be provided by the researchers. Here we see the opportunity cost come into play: teachers will likely get better results from planning and implementing the strategies we've covered elsewhere in this book than from replicating the studies and thinking of keywords that will fit within these techniques.

Why are keyword mnemonic and imagery for text less useful strategies?

As with highlighting, these strategies require the learner to do some extra work – creating the mnemonic/image – but the quality of the retention will depend on the quality of the imagery. For example, the benefit of getting students to create a mnemonic for foreign words is limited if the students' primary language vocabulary is limited. Both these strategies are also restricted to imagery-friendly materials: abstract or complex content cannot be easily imagined (in subjects such as maths or physics, for example). There's also an age limitation: these strategies are much harder to use with younger students or students who have weak background knowledge owing to their lack of vocabulary development and ability to understand complex materials.

Further reading

Practice testing

Agarwal, P.K., Roediger, H.L., McDaniel. M.A. & McDermott, K.B. (2020) *How to Use Retrieval Practice to Improve Learning*, Washington University in St Louis, www.retrievalpractice.org

Education Endowment Foundation. (2021) *Cognitive Science Approaches in the Classroom: a review of the evidence*, https://educationendowmentfoundation.org.uk/education-evidence/evidence-reviews/cognitive-science-approaches-in-the-classroom

Fazio, L.K. & Agarwal, P.K. (2020) *How to Implement Retrieval-Based Learning in Early Childhood Education*, Vanderbilt University, www.retrievalpractice.org

Pan, S.C. & Agarwal, P.K. (2020) *Retrieval Practice and Transfer of Learning: fostering students' application of knowledge*, UC San Diego, www.retrievalpractice.org

Pashler, H., Bain, P.M., Bottge, B.A., Graesser, A., Koedinger, K., McDaniel, M. & Metcalfe, J. (2007) *Organizing Instruction and Study to Improve Student Learning: IES practice guide*, National Center for Education Research, https://files.eric.ed.gov/fulltext/ED498555.pdf

Smith, M. & Weinstein, Y. (2016) "Learn how to study using... retrieval practice", *The Learning Scientists*, www.learningscientists.org/blog/2016/6/23-1

Distributed practice

Carpenter, S.K. & Agarwal, P.K. (2020) *How to Use Spaced Retrieval Practice to Boost Learning*, Iowa State University, www.retrievalpractice.org

Education Endowment Foundation. (2021) *Cognitive Science Approaches in the Classroom: a review of the evidence*, https://educationendowmentfoundation.org.uk/education-evidence/evidence-reviews/cognitive-science-approaches-in-the-classroom

Hughes, C.A. & Lee, J. (2019) "Effective approaches for scheduling and formatting practice: distributed, cumulative, and interleaved practice", *Teaching Exceptional Children*, 51:6

Pashler, H., Bain, P.M., Bottge, B.A., Graesser, A., Koedinger, K., McDaniel, M. & Metcalfe, J. (2007) *Organizing Instruction and Study to Improve Student Learning: IES practice guide*, National Center for Education Research, https://files.eric.ed.gov/fulltext/ED498555.pdf

Weinstein, Y. & Smith, M. (2016) "Learn how to study using... spaced practice", *The Learning Scientists*, www.learningscientists.org/blog/2016/7/21-1

Interleaving

Education Endowment Foundation. (2021) *Cognitive Science Approaches in the Classroom: a review of the evidence*, https://educationendowmentfoundation.org.uk/ education-evidence/evidence-reviews/cognitive-science-approaches-in-the-classroom

Hughes, C.A. & Lee, J. (2019) "Effective approaches for scheduling and formatting practice: distributed, cumulative, and interleaved practice", *Teaching Exceptional Children*, 51:6

Rohrer, D., Dedrick, R.F. & Agarwal, P.K. (2017) *Interleaved Mathematics Practice: giving students a chance to learn what they need to know*, www.retrievalpractice.org

Rohrer, D. & Taylor, K. (2007) "The shuffling of mathematics problems improves learning", *Instructional Science*, 35, 481-498

Taylor, K. & Rohrer, D. (2010) "The effects of interleaved practice", *Applied Cognitive Psychology*, 24:6, 837-848

Weinstein, Y. & Smith, M. (2016) "Learn to study using... interleaving", *The Learning Scientists*, www.learningscientists.org/blog/2016/8/11-1

Elaborative interrogation and self-explanation

Gilbert, K. (2016) "Self-explanation as a study strategy for math", *The Learning Scientists*, www.learningscientists.org/blog/2016/7/12-1

Kirschner, P.A., Neelen, M., Hoof, T. & Surma, T. (2021) "Let's get to work with productive learning strategies: summarising", *3-Star Learning Experiences* (blog), https://3starlearningexperiences.wordpress.com/2021/03/23/lets-get-to-work-with-productive-learning-strategies-summarising

Loughborough University Mathematics Education Centre. (n.d.) *Self-Explanation Training for Mathematics Students*, www.lboro.ac.uk/media/media/schoolanddepartments/ mathematics-education-centre/downloads/research/SE-booklet.pdf

Pashler, H., Bain, P.M., Bottge, B.A., Graesser, A., Koedinger, K., McDaniel, M. & Metcalfe, J. (2007) *Organizing Instruction and Study to Improve Student Learning: IES practice guide*, National Center for Education Research, https://files.eric.ed.gov/fulltext/ ED498555.pdf

Pershan, M. (2021) "Good explanations connect particulars to principles", Blog, http:// notepad.michaelpershan.com/good-explanations-connect-particulars-to-principles

Smith, M. & Weinstein, Y. (2016) "Learn how to study using... elaboration", *The Learning Scientists*, www.learningscientists.org/blog/2016/7/7-1

CHAPTER 3

A WORD OF CAUTION

'Educational improvement cannot be directed towards a static ideal state, but requires constant monitoring, fine-tuning and "shepherding" in order to secure outcomes such as high equity and high attainment … It is not constant arbitrary "tinkering"'[145]

To close this book, I want to reflect on a few ideas…

When a tree is cut off from its roots, the branches will wither and die

This book is intended to act as a companion to Dunlosky's original paper and a helpful starting point for thinking about the strategies in further detail. In order to communicate the complex ideas within the parameters of a book of this size, certain nuances and details have not been thoroughly explored. Furthermore, some of the analogies and concrete examples that we've considered are helpful in communicating these complex ideas, but by their very nature are context-specific and so run the risk of oversimplification. Therefore, we must take the time to understand the existing evidence when we think about the strategies and how they translate to the classroom. This includes looking at the mechanisms underpinning the strategy, examining the contexts in which it's already been tested and carefully planning any changes to our practice. We should take the time to analyse the problem we're trying to solve and pay attention to its root causes, otherwise we run the risk of getting caught in Frank Achtenhagen's "cycle of planned failure", illustrated by figure 8 on the next page.

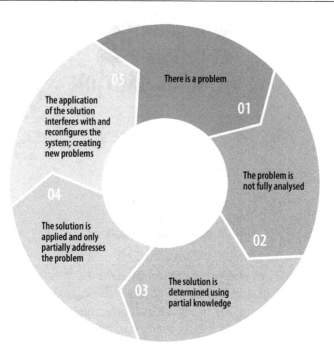

Figure 8. Frank Achtenhagen's cycle of planned failure.[146]

There are very few 'bad' strategies, but there are many bad uses for any given strategy

We must be clear on what we're trying to achieve and then select the most appropriate strategy: clarity of purpose is key. For example, it may be unwise to try to force interleaving into situations where the goal is something other than recognising similarities and differences between related ideas. Similarly, we shouldn't throw out our highlighters, but rather understand that they serve a very specific purpose and approach any suggestion that we use them for another purpose with extreme caution.

The Education Endowment Foundation has put together an excellent guide on how schools can effectively implement changes to existing practice, which you can download here: bit.ly/EEFImplementation. Figure 9 illustrates the EEF's implementation process.

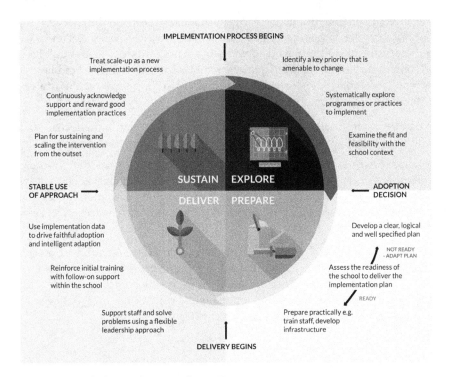

IMPLEMENTATION PROCESS BEGINS

Treat scale-up as a new implementation process

Identify a key priority that is amenable to change

Continuously acknowledge support and reward good implementation practices

Systematically explore programmes or practices to implement

Plan for sustaining and scaling the intervention from the outset

Examine the fit and feasibility with the school context

STABLE USE OF APPROACH

SUSTAIN EXPLORE

DELIVER PREPARE

ADOPTION DECISION

Use implementation data to drive faithful adoption and intelligent adaption

Develop a clear, logical and well specified plan

NOT READY - ADAPT PLAN

Reinforce initial training with follow-on support within the school

Assess the readiness of the school to deliver the implementation plan

READY

Support staff and solve problems using a flexible leadership approach

Prepare practically e.g. train staff, develop infrastructure

DELIVERY BEGINS

Figure 9. The EEF's implementation process diagram.[147]

As we don't have enough space in this book to unpack effective implementation, I urge you to read the EEF's full guidance. In the meantime, I'll draw your attention to the first phase of the EEF's implementation process: explore. We should be wary of starting from a point of "This looks like a good approach – let's try it". Such "arbitrary tinkering"[148] is likely to be a poor use of time at best and, at worst, actively harmful to students' learning. Instead, we must start with the problem we're trying to address, then rigorously *explore* the evidence in order to discern what solution best matches the context before attempting implementation.

Challenge is an essential part of learning, but not all challenges are helpful

As we've seen, effortful processes are an inherent part of effective learning and this is the reason why testing can have bigger benefits than underlining. However, we don't want to mindlessly quiz students in every lesson because it's "retrieval practice" – if students have nothing to retrieve then they won't get much practice of anything! Similarly, quizzing on the same things every day doesn't allow for forgetting, which can be harnessed to deepen learning. We do want students to think hard about their learning, so we need to think hard about how and when we'll use quizzes, what their content will be, and how to appropriately adjust the difficulty so students reap the benefits of the strategy without becoming demotivated.

'Lead by example. It's not enough to teach your students the techniques and then tell them to use them. You need to use them yourself'[149]

In an ideal world, we would give our students a stack of flashcards, a calendar telling them exactly when to revise which topics and a session on effective ways of studying, and they would all go away and religiously use those tools and information. However, we know this would be a significant challenge, for a vast number of reasons.

So, although it's crucial to guide our students towards stronger study strategies and away from weaker ones, it's perhaps even more crucial to ensure our own classroom practices mirror our advice. We must practise what we preach – not just because leading by example is an inherently good thing to do, but because our students are the ones who stand to benefit.

REFERENCES

1   Guru Granth Sahib, ang 317

2   Dunlosky, J. (2013) "Strengthening the student toolbox: study strategies to boost learning", *American Educator*, 37:3, 12-21, p.12

3   Dunlosky, J., Rawson, K., Marsh, E., Nathan, M. & Willingham, D. (2013) "Improving students' learning with effective learning techniques: promising directions from cognitive and educational psychology", *Psychological Science in the Public Interest*, 14:1, 4-58, p.5

4   Dunlosky, J. (2013) "Strengthening the student toolbox: study strategies to boost learning", *American Educator*, 37:3, 12-21, p.13

5   Ibid.

6   Fletcher-Wood, H. (2019) "Forming good habits, breaking bad habits: what works?", *Improving Teaching* (blog), https://improvingteaching.co.uk/2019/01/13/forming-good-habits-breaking-bad-habits-what-works

7   Wiliam, D. (2013) *Redesigning Schooling 3: principled curriculum design*, SSAT, p.19

8   Dunlosky, J., Rawson, K., Marsh, E., Nathan, M. & Willingham, D. (2013) "Improving students' learning with effective learning techniques: promising directions from cognitive and educational psychology", *Psychological Science in the Public Interest*, 14:1, 4-58, p.7

9   Tierney, S. (2021) "5 evidence based papers all teachers should read (updated)", *Leading Learner* (blog), https://leadinglearner.me/2021/03/14/5-evidenced-based-papers-all-teachers-should-read-updated

10   Kromann, C.B., Jensen, M.L. & Ringsted, C. (2009) "The effect of testing on skills learning", *Medical Education*, 43:1, 21-27

11   Koh, K. & Meyer, D.E. (1991) "Function learning: induction of continuous stimulus-response relations", *Journal of Experimental Psychology: Learning, Memory, and Cognition*, 17:5, 811-836

12   Dunlosky, J., Rawson, K., Marsh, E., Nathan, M. & Willingham, D. (2013) "Improving students' learning with effective learning techniques: promising directions from cognitive and educational psychology", *Psychological Science in the Public Interest*, 14:1, 4-58

13   Ibid.

14   Ibid.

15   Ibid.

16   Ibid.

17   Ibid.

18   Ibid.

19   Ibid., p.19

20   Ibid.

21   Ibid.

22   Bjork, E.L. & Bjork, R.A. (2011) "Making things hard on yourself, but in a good way: creating desirable difficulties to enhance learning", in M.A. Gernsbacher et al. (eds.) *Psychology and the Real World: essays illustrating fundamental contributions to society*, Worth Publishers, p.57

23   Didau, D. & Rose, N. (2016) *What Every Teacher Needs to Know About Psychology*, John Catt Educational

24   Willingham, D.T. (2021) *Why Don't Students Like School?* (second edition), Jossey-Bass

25   Rose, N. (2020) "Understanding memory", in *The Early Career Framework Handbook*, SAGE, pp.35-44

26   Willingham, D.T. (2021) *Why Don't Students Like School?* (second edition), Jossey-Bass

27   Ibid.

28   Didau, D. & Rose, N. (2016) *What Every Teacher Needs to Know About Psychology*, John Catt Educational

29   Kirschner, P., Sweller, J. & Clark, R. (2006) "Why minimal guidance during instruction does not work: an analysis of the failure of constructivist, discovery, problem-based, experiential, and inquiry-based teaching", *Educational Psychologist*, 41:2, 75-86

30   Rose, N. (2020) "Understanding memory", in *The Early Career Framework Handbook*, SAGE, pp.35-44

31   Mccrea, P. (2017) *Memorable Teaching*

32   Didau, D. & Rose, N. (2016) *What Every Teacher Needs to Know About Psychology*, John Catt Educational, p.57

33   Roediger, H., Weinstein, Y. & Agarwal, P.K. (2010) "Forgetting: preliminary considerations", in S. Della Sala (ed.) *Forgetting*, Psychology Press

34   Ibid.

35   Adapted from Didau, D. & Rose, N. (2016) *What Every Teacher Needs to Know About Psychology*, John Catt Educational, p.55

36   Bjork, R.A. & Bjork, E.L. (1992) "A new theory of disuse and an old theory of stimulus fluctuation", in A. Healy et al. (eds.) *From Learning Processes to Cognitive Processes: essays in honor of William K. Estes* (vol. 2), Erlbaum, pp. 35-67

37   Ibid.

38   Ibid.

39   Adapted from Yan, V. (2016) "Retrieval strength vs. storage strength", *The Learning Scientists*, www.learningscientists.org/blog/2016/5/10-1

40   Dunlosky, J. (2013) "Strengthening the student toolbox: study strategies to boost learning", *American Educator*, 37:3, 12-21, p.20

41   Kirschner, P.A. & Hendrick, C. (2020) *How Learning Happens: seminal works in educational psychology and what they mean in practice*, Routledge, p.x

42   Roediger, H.L. & Karpicke, J.D. (2006) "Test-enhanced learning: taking memory tests improves long-term retention", *Psychological Science*, 17:3 via Roediger, H.L. & Pyc, M.A. (2012) "Inexpensive techniques to improve education: applying cognitive psychology to enhance educational practice", *Journal of Applied Research in Memory and Cognition*, 1:4, 242-248

43   Ibid.

44   Dunlosky, J. (2013) "Strengthening the student toolbox: study strategies to boost learning", *American Educator*, 37:3, 12-21

45   Dunlosky, J., Rawson, K., Marsh, E., Nathan, M. & Willingham, D. (2013) "Improving students' learning with effective learning techniques: promising directions from cognitive and educational psychology", *Psychological Science in the Public Interest*, 14:1, 4-58

46   Dunlosky, J. (2013) "Strengthening the student toolbox: study strategies to boost learning", *American Educator*, 37:3, 12-21

47   Willingham, D.T. (2008) "What will improve a student's memory?", *American Educator*, 32:4, 17-25, p.17

48   Bjork, R.A. & Bjork, E.L. (1992) "A new theory of disuse and an old theory of stimulus fluctuation", in A. Healy et al. (eds.) *From Learning Processes to Cognitive Processes: essays in honor of William K. Estes* (vol. 2), Erlbaum, pp. 35-67, p.37

49   Dunlosky, J., Rawson, K., Marsh, E., Nathan, M. & Willingham, D. (2013) "Improving students' learning with effective learning techniques: promising directions from cognitive and educational psychology", *Psychological Science in the Public Interest*, 14:1, 4-58

50   Mccrea, P. (2017) *Memorable Teaching*

51   Bjork, R.A. & Bjork, E.L. (1992) "A new theory of disuse and an old theory of stimulus fluctuation", in A. Healy et al. (eds.) *From Learning Processes to Cognitive Processes: essays in honor of William K. Estes* (vol. 2), Erlbaum, pp. 35-67

52   Fiechter, J.L. & Benjamin, A.S. (2018) "Diminishing-cues retrieval practice: a memory-enhancing technique that works when regular testing doesn't", *Psychonomic Bulletin & Review*, 25:5, 1868-1876

53   Ibid.

54   Dunlosky, J., Rawson, K., Marsh, E., Nathan, M. & Willingham, D. (2013) "Improving students' learning with effective learning techniques: promising directions from cognitive and educational psychology", *Psychological Science in the Public Interest*, 14:1, 4-58

55   Butler, A.C. & Roediger, H.L. (2008) "Feedback enhances the positive effects and reduces the negative effects of multiple-choice testing", *Memory & Cognition*, 36:3, 604-616

56   Didau, D. & Rose, N. (2016) *What Every Teacher Needs to Know About Psychology*, John Catt Educational

57   Bjork, R.A. & Bjork, E.L. (2019) "Forgetting as the friend of learning: implications for teaching and self-regulated learning", *Advances in Physiology Education*, 43:2, 164-167, p.164

58 Bjork, R.A. & Bjork, E.L. (1992) "A new theory of disuse and an old theory of stimulus fluctuation", in A. Healy et al. (eds.) *From Learning Processes to Cognitive Processes: essays in honor of William K. Estes* (vol. 2), Erlbaum, pp. 35-67

59 Dunlosky, J. (2013) "Strengthening the student toolbox: study strategies to boost learning", *American Educator*, 37:3, 12-21

60 Bloom, K.C. & Shuell, T.J. (1981) "Effects of massed and distributed practice on the learning and retention of second-language vocabulary", *The Journal of Educational Research*, 74:4, 245-248
    via
    Roediger, H.L. & Pyc, M.A. (2012) "Inexpensive techniques to improve education: applying cognitive psychology to enhance educational practice", *Journal of Applied Research in Memory and Cognition*, 1:4, 242-248

61 Ibid.

62 Dunlosky, J. (2013) "Strengthening the student toolbox: study strategies to boost learning", *American Educator*, 37:3, 12-21, p.16

63 Ibid.

64 Bjork, R.A. & Bjork, E.L. (2019) "Forgetting as the friend of learning: implications for teaching and self-regulated learning", *Advances in Physiology Education*, 43:2, 164-167, p.164

65 Dunlosky, J., Rawson, K., Marsh, E., Nathan, M. & Willingham, D. (2013) "Improving students' learning with effective learning techniques: promising directions from cognitive and educational psychology", *Psychological Science in the Public Interest*, 14:1, 4-58,

66 Adapted from www.repetico.com/faq-general

67 Didau, D. & Rose, N. (2016) *What Every Teacher Needs to Know About Psychology*, John Catt Educational, p.57

68 Bjork, R.A. & Bjork, E.L. (1992) "A new theory of disuse and an old theory of stimulus fluctuation", in A. Healy et al. (eds.) *From Learning Processes to Cognitive Processes: essays in honor of William K. Estes* (vol. 2), Erlbaum

69 Ibid.

70 Dunlosky, J., Rawson, K., Marsh, E., Nathan, M. & Willingham, D. (2013) "Improving students' learning with effective learning techniques: promising directions from cognitive and educational psychology", *Psychological Science in the Public Interest*, 14:1, 4-58

71 Willingham, D.T. (2002) "Allocating student study time: 'massed' versus 'distributed' practice", *American Educator*, Summer, www.aft.org/periodical/american-educator/summer-2002/ask-cognitive-scientist

72 Dunlosky, J., Rawson, K., Marsh, E., Nathan, M. & Willingham, D. (2013) "Improving students' learning with effective learning techniques: promising directions from cognitive and educational psychology", *Psychological Science in the Public Interest*, 14:1, 4-58

73 Rosenshine, B. (2012) "Principles of instruction: research-based strategies that all teachers should know", *American Educator*, 36:1, 12-39

74 Ibid.

75 Dunlosky, J., Rawson, K., Marsh, E., Nathan, M. & Willingham, D. (2013) "Improving students' learning with effective learning techniques: promising directions from cognitive and educational psychology", *Psychological Science in the Public Interest*, 14:1, 4-58, p.35

76 Willingham, D.T. (2002) "Allocating student study time: 'massed' versus 'distributed' practice", *American Educator*, Summer, www.aft.org/periodical/american-educator/ summer-2002/ask-cognitive-scientist

77 Rohrer, D. (2009) "The effects of spacing and mixing practice problems", *Journal for Research in Mathematics Education*, 40:1, 4-17

78 Dunlosky, J., Rawson, K., Marsh, E., Nathan, M. & Willingham, D. (2013) "Improving students' learning with effective learning techniques: promising directions from cognitive and educational psychology", *Psychological Science in the Public Interest*, 14:1, 4-58

79 Ibid.

80 Willingham, D.T. (2002) "Allocating student study time: 'massed' versus 'distributed' practice", *American Educator*, Summer, www.aft.org/periodical/american-educator/ summer-2002/ask-cognitive-scientist

81 Cepeda, N.J., Vul, E., Rohrer, D., Wixted, J.T. & Pashler, H. (2008) "Spacing effects in learning: a temporal ridgeline of optimal retention", *Psychological Science*, 19:11, 1095-1102

82 Kirschner, P.A. & Hendrick, C. (2020) *How Learning Happens: seminal works in educational psychology and what they mean in practice*, Routledge, p.18

83 Taylor, K. & Rohrer, D. (2010) "The effects of interleaved practice", *Applied Cognitive Psychology*, 24:6, 837-848
   via
   Roediger, H.L. & Pyc, M.A. (2012) "Inexpensive techniques to improve education: applying cognitive psychology to enhance educational practice", *Journal of Applied Research in Memory and Cognition*, 1:4, 242-248

84 Ibid.

85 Perry, T., Lea, R., Jørgensen, C.R., Cordingley, P., Shapiro, K. & Youdell, D. (2021) *Cognitive Science in the Classroom: evidence and practice review*, Education Endowment Foundation, https://educationendowmentfoundation.org.uk/ education-evidence/evidence-reviews/cognitive-science-approaches-in-the-classroom

86 Dunlosky, J., Rawson, K., Marsh, E., Nathan, M. & Willingham, D. (2013) "Improving students' learning with effective learning techniques: promising directions from cognitive and educational psychology", *Psychological Science in the Public Interest*, 14:1, 4-58

87 Dunlosky, J. (2013) "Strengthening the student toolbox: study strategies to boost learning", *American Educator*, 37:3, 12-21

88 Taylor, K. & Rohrer, D. (2010) "The effects of interleaved practice", *Applied Cognitive Psychology*, 24:6, 837-848

89   Perry, T., Lea, R., Jørgensen, C.R., Cordingley, P., Shapiro, K. & Youdell, D. (2021) *Cognitive Science Approaches in the Classroom: a review of the evidence*, Education Endowment Foundation, https://bit.ly/3KUVBcX

90   Dunlosky, J., Rawson, K., Marsh, E., Nathan, M. & Willingham, D. (2013) "Improving students' learning with effective learning techniques: promising directions from cognitive and educational psychology", *Psychological Science in the Public Interest*, 14:1, 4-58

91   Ibid.

92   Taylor, K. & Rohrer, D. (2010) "The effects of interleaved practice", *Applied Cognitive Psychology*, 24:6, 837-848

93   Carvalho, P.F. & Goldstone, R.L. (2019) "When does interleaving practice improve learning?", in J. Dunlosky & K.A. Rawson (eds.), *The Cambridge Handbook of Cognition and Education*, Cambridge University Press, 411-436

94   Dunlosky, J., Rawson, K., Marsh, E., Nathan, M. & Willingham, D. (2013) "Improving students' learning with effective learning techniques: promising directions from cognitive and educational psychology", *Psychological Science in the Public Interest*, 14:1, 4-58

95   Ibid.

96   Kang, S.H. & Pashler, H. (2012) "Learning painting styles: spacing is advantageous when it promotes discriminative contrast", *Applied Cognitive Psychology*, 26:1, 97-103

97   Effectiviology. (n.d.) "Interleaving: how mixed practice can boost learning", https://effectiviology.com/interleaving

98   Stambaugh, L. (2009) "When repetition isn't the best practice strategy: examining differing levels of contextual interference during practice", *Proceedings of the International Symposium on Performance Science, Auckland, New Zealand*, European Association of Conservatoires

99   Samani, J. & Pan, S.C. (2021) "Interleaved practice enhances memory and problem-solving ability in undergraduate physics", *NPJ Science of Learning*, 6:1, 1-11

100   Dunlosky, J. (2013) "Strengthening the student toolbox: study strategies to boost learning", *American Educator*, 37:3, 12-21

101   Effectiviology. (n.d.) "Interleaving: how mixed practice can boost learning", https://effectiviology.com/interleaving

102   Kang, S.H. & Pashler, H. (2012) "Learning painting styles: spacing is advantageous when it promotes discriminative contrast", *Applied Cognitive Psychology*, 26:1, 97-103

103   Dunlosky, J. (2013) "Strengthening the student toolbox: study strategies to boost learning", *American Educator*, 37:3, 12-21

104   Ibid., p.18

105   Ibid., p.18

106   Renkl, A. & Eitel, A. (2019) "Self-explaining: learning about principles and their application", in J. Dunlosky & K.A. Rawson (eds.), *The Cambridge Handbook of Cognition and Education*, Cambridge University Press, pp.528-549

107 Pershan, M. (2021) "Good explanations connect particulars to principles", Blog, http://notepad.michaelpershan.com/good-explanations-connect-particulars-to-principles

108 Dunlosky, J. (2013) "Strengthening the student toolbox: study strategies to boost learning", *American Educator*, 37:3, 12-21

109 Ibid.

110 Dunlosky, J., Rawson, K., Marsh, E., Nathan, M. & Willingham, D. (2013) "Improving students' learning with effective learning techniques: promising directions from cognitive and educational psychology", *Psychological Science in the Public Interest*, 14:1, 4-58

111 Willoughby, T. & Wood, E. (1994) "Elaborative interrogation examined at encoding and retrieval", *Learning and Instruction*, 4:2, 139-149

112 Dunlosky, J., Rawson, K., Marsh, E., Nathan, M. & Willingham, D. (2013) "Improving students' learning with effective learning techniques: promising directions from cognitive and educational psychology", *Psychological Science in the Public Interest*, 14:1, 4-58

113 Dunlosky, J. (2013) "Strengthening the student toolbox: study strategies to boost learning", *American Educator*, 37:3, 12-21

114 Pershan, M. (2021) "Good explanations connect particulars to principles", Blog, http://notepad.michaelpershan.com/good-explanations-connect-particulars-to-principles

115 Kingsbridge Research School. (2019) "Elaborative interrogation", https://researchschool.org.uk/kingsbridge/news/elaborative-interrogation

116 The Learning Scientists. (2017) "Episode 6 – elaborative interrogation" (podcast), www.learningscientists.org/learning-scientists-podcast/2017/11/1/episode-6-elaborative-interrogation

117 Kingsbridge Research School. (2019) "Elaborative interrogation", https://researchschool.org.uk/kingsbridge/news/elaborative-interrogation

118 Dunlosky, J., Rawson, K., Marsh, E., Nathan, M. & Willingham, D. (2013) "Improving students' learning with effective learning techniques: promising directions from cognitive and educational psychology", *Psychological Science in the Public Interest*, 14:1, 4-58

119 Pashler, H., Bain, P.M., Bottge, B.A., Graesser, A., Koedinger, K., McDaniel, M. & Metcalfe, J. (2007) *Organizing Instruction and Study to Improve Student Learning: IES practice guide*, National Center for Education Research, https://files.eric.ed.gov/fulltext/ED498555.pdf

120 Dunlosky, J. (2013) "Strengthening the student toolbox: study strategies to boost learning", *American Educator*, 37:3, 12-21

121 https://twitter.com/dylanwiliam/status/1146539918128291841

122 Dunlosky, J., Rawson, K., Marsh, E., Nathan, M. & Willingham, D. (2013) "Improving students' learning with effective learning techniques: promising directions from cognitive and educational psychology", *Psychological Science in the Public Interest*, 14:1, 4-58

123 Dunlosky, J. (2013) "Strengthening the student toolbox: study strategies to boost learning", *American Educator*, 37:3, 12-21

124 Kirschner, P.A., Neelen, M., Hoof, T. & Surma, T. (2021) "Let's get to work with productive learning strategies: summarising", *3-Star Learning Experiences* (blog), https://3starlearningexperiences.wordpress.com/2021/03/23/lets-get-to-work-with-productive-learning-strategies-summarising

125 Dunlosky, J., Rawson, K., Marsh, E., Nathan, M. & Willingham, D. (2013) "Improving students' learning with effective learning techniques: promising directions from cognitive and educational psychology", *Psychological Science in the Public Interest*, 14:1, 4-58

126 Shing, Y.L. & Brod, G. (2016) "Effects of prior knowledge on memory: implications for education", *Mind, Brain, and Education*, 10:3, 153-161

127 Dunlosky, J., Rawson, K., Marsh, E., Nathan, M. & Willingham, D. (2013) "Improving students' learning with effective learning techniques: promising directions from cognitive and educational psychology", *Psychological Science in the Public Interest*, 14:1, 4-58

128 Fiorella, L. & Mayer, R.E. (2016) "Eight ways to promote generative learning", *Educational Psychology Review*, 28, 717-741

129 Kirschner, P.A., Neelen, M., Hoof, T. & Surma, T. (2021) "Let's get to work with productive learning strategies: summarising", *3-Star Learning Experiences* (blog), https://3starlearningexperiences.wordpress.com/2021/03/23/lets-get-to-work-with-productive-learning-strategies-summarising

130 Dunlosky, J., Rawson, K., Marsh, E., Nathan, M. & Willingham, D. (2013) "Improving students' learning with effective learning techniques: promising directions from cognitive and educational psychology", *Psychological Science in the Public Interest*, 14:1, 4-58

131 Fiorella, L. & Mayer, R.E. (2016) "Eight ways to promote generative learning", *Educational Psychology Review*, 28, 717-741

132 Hattie, J., Biggs, J. & Purdie, N. (1996) "Effects of learning skills interventions on student learning: a meta-analysis", *Review of Educational Research*, 66:2, 99-136

133 Dunlosky, J., Rawson, K., Marsh, E., Nathan, M. & Willingham, D. (2013) "Improving students' learning with effective learning techniques: promising directions from cognitive and educational psychology", *Psychological Science in the Public Interest*, 14:1, 4-58

134 Dunlosky, J. (2013) "Strengthening the student toolbox: study strategies to boost learning", *American Educator*, 37:3, 12-21

135 Association for Psychological Science. (2013) "Q&A with psychological scientist John Dunlosky", www.psychologicalscience.org/publications/observer/obsonline/qa-with-psychological-scientist-john-dunlosky.html

136 Dunlosky, J. (2013) "Strengthening the student toolbox: study strategies to boost learning", *American Educator*, 37:3, 12-21, p.20

137 Association for Psychological Science. (2013) "Q&A with psychological scientist John Dunlosky", www.psychologicalscience.org/publications/observer/obsonline/qa-with-psychological-scientist-john-dunlosky.html

138 Dunlosky, J. (2013) "Strengthening the student toolbox: study strategies to boost learning", *American Educator*, 37:3, 12-21

139 Ibid.

140 Dunlosky, J. (2013) "Strengthening the student toolbox: study strategies to boost learning", *American Educator*, 37:3, 12-21

141 Dunlosky, J., Rawson, K., Marsh, E., Nathan, M. & Willingham, D. (2013) "Improving students' learning with effective learning techniques: promising directions from cognitive and educational psychology", *Psychological Science in the Public Interest*, 14:1, 4-58

142 Ibid.

143 Leutner, D., Leopold, C. & Sumfleth, E. (2009) "Cognitive load and science text comprehension: effects of drawing and mentally imagining text content", *Computers in Human Behavior*, 25:2, 284-289

144 Ibid.

145 Cambridge Assessment. (2017) *A Cambridge Approach to Improving Education: using International insights to manage complexity*, p.9, www.cambridgeassessment. org.uk/Images/cambridge-approach-to-improving-education.pdf

146 Achtenhagen, F. (1994) Presentation to Third International Conference of Learning at Work, Milan, June 1994
via
Cambridge Assessment. (2017) *A Cambridge Approach to Improving Education: using International insights to manage complexity*, p.12, www.cambridgeassessment. org.uk/Images/cambridge-approach-to-improving-education.pdf

147 Sharples, J., Albers, B., Fraser, S. & Kime, S. (2019) *Putting Evidence to Work: a school's guide to implementation – guidance report*, Education Endowment Foundation, p.5, https://bit.ly/EEFImplementation

148 Cambridge Assessment. (2017) *A Cambridge Approach to Improving Education: using International insights to manage complexity*, p.10, www.cambridgeassessment. org.uk/Images/cambridge-approach-to-improving-education.pdf

149 Kirschner, P.A. & Hendrick, C. (2020) *How Learning Happens: seminal works in educational psychology and what they mean in practice*, Routledge, p.214